The 1921 Tulsa Race Massacre

The 1921 Tulsa Race Massacre

A Photographic History

Karlos K. Hill

Foreword by
Kevin Matthews

UNIVERSITY OF
OKLAHOMA PRESS
NORMAN

KARLOS K. HILL
General Editor

LIBRARY OF CONGRESS
CATALOGING-IN-PUBLICATION DATA

Names: Hill, Karlos K., author.
Title: The 1921 Tulsa Race Massacre:
A Photographic History / Karlos K. Hill.
Description: Norman : University of
Oklahoma Press, [2021] | Includes
bibliographical references and index. |
Summary: "A visual documentary account
of the violence unleashed upon the Black
citizens of Tulsa, Oklahoma, in 1921, using
over one hundred color photos and oral
history testimony"—Provided by publisher.
Identifiers: LCCN 2020032960 |
ISBN 978-0-8061-6856-2 (hardcover)
Subjects: LCSH: Tulsa Race Massacre,
Tulsa, Okla., 1921—Pictorial works. |
African Americans—Violence against—
Oklahoma—Tulsa—History—20th century. |
Greenwood (Tulsa, Okla.)—Race relations—
History—20th century. | Tulsa (Okla.)—Race
relations—History—20th century. | LCGFT:
Photobooks.
Classification: LCC F704.T92 H55 2021 | DDC
976.6/8600496073—dc23
LC record available at https://lccn.loc..
gov/2020032960

The paper in this book meets the guidelines for
permanence and durability of the Committee
on Production Guidelines for Book Longevity
of the Council on Library Resources, Inc. ∞

The 1921 Tulsa Race Massacre: A Photographic
History is Volume 1 in The Greenwood Cultural
Center Series in African Diaspora History
and Culture.

1 2 3 4 5 6 7 8 9 10

To the victims and survivors of the 1921 Tulsa Race Massacre

Introduction

Race Riot or Race Massacre?

The unprejudiced and indirectly interested people have from the beginning referred to the affair as the "race riot," others with deeper feeling refer to it as a "massacre," while many who would saddle the blame upon the negro, have used the designation, artfully coined, "negro uprising." After six months work among them, it has been found the majority of the negroes who were the greatest sufferers refer to June 1st, 1921 as "the time of dewa." Whatever people choose to call it, the word or phrase has not yet been coined which can adequately describe the events of June 1st last. This report refers to the tragedy as a "disaster."

MAURICE WILLOWS
Director of Disaster Relief
Tulsa County American Red Cross
December 31, 1921

Willows quoted in Hannibal B. Johnson, *Black Wall Street: From Riot to Renaissance in Tulsa's Historic Greenwood District* (Fort Worth: Eakin Press, 1998), 98.

DURING THE EARLY TWENTIETH CENTURY, the Greenwood District of Tulsa, Oklahoma, was known as the "Negro Wall Street of America" because of its prosperous Black business community. In 1921, Greenwood was home to nearly eleven thousand Black people—one-tenth of Tulsa's overall population—and spanned a thirty-five-block area. (See map 1.) The district boasted close to two hundred businesses, including thirty-one restaurants, more than two dozen grocery stores, five hotels, four drugstores, and two theaters. There were a dozen churches, as well as two schools, two hospitals, two newspapers, and a public library.[1] Most of the businesses and residential properties were owned by Black Tulsans.[2] The Black professional class comprised not only clergy and teachers but also three lawyers, including the pioneering Buck Colbert Franklin; fifteen doctors, one of whom was a nationally acclaimed surgeon, Dr. A. C. Jackson; and enterprising businessmen such as Greenwood's founder, O. W. Gurley.[3] Remarkably, the neighborhood's affluence occurred at a time when most Black southerners lived in rural areas and toiled as sharecroppers on white-owned plantations. For all these reasons, the Greenwood District was not just a wealthy Black community in the age of segregation; it was, and remains, a potent symbol of Black excellence. The eruption of white mob violence in downtown Tulsa on May 31, 1921, interrupted Greenwood's historic ascendancy.

What has come to be known as the 1921 Tulsa Race Massacre was instigated by speculation that nineteen-year-old Dick Rowland, who was Black, had attacked Sarah Page, a seventeen-year-old white elevator operator. While it is unclear precisely what occurred during the brief interaction between the two in an elevator in Tulsa's downtown business district on May 30, we know that Page screamed and Rowland fled the elevator in a panic. There is no record of what Page told bystanders or the police who interviewed her following the incident, but police authorities were left with the impression that Rowland had attacked her.[4]

The following afternoon, on May 31, the *Tulsa Tribune* published an incendiary article, "Nab Negro for Attacking Girl in an Elevator," which asserted that Rowland had indeed assaulted Page.[5] As was common for the era, the *Tribune* insinuated that he had attempted to rape her.[6] Word began to spread about the alleged attack, and by evening a large number of whites had begun to gather in front of the Tulsa County Courthouse, where Rowland was being held in the county jail. It quickly became clear that some among the crowd intended to lynch him.[7]

Fearing that the lynching of Dick Rowland was imminent, a small, armed contingent of Black men, some of whom had served in World War I, came to the courthouse around 9:00 P.M. to offer the authorities their assistance. They left upon being promised that no harm would come to Rowland, but their brief presence further enraged the growing white mob. By 9:30 there were almost two thousand angry whites milling around outside the courthouse, many with guns, and the county sheriff was preparing his deputies to make a stand should the building be attacked. When a second, larger group of Black men arrived in hopes of helping to protect Rowland, they were again told that their services were not needed. This time, however, a white bystander, perhaps angered by the sight of Black men carrying weapons, attempted to take the gun of a Black veteran who was walking away with the rest of the group. As the men struggled, one of their guns went off. In the chaos of the moment, armed whites began shooting indiscriminately at the retreating Black men, some of whom shot back. In that first quick interchange of gunfire, twenty people were killed or wounded. The Black men hastily left the scene, but they were followed by armed whites, who engaged them in further gunfire on Fourth Street and then on Cincinnati Avenue, resulting in additional casualties. That initial pursuit ended when what was left of the group of Black men made it across the tracks of the Saint Louis–San Francisco Railway (popularly known as the Frisco Railroad), the demarcation line between white Tulsa and Black Tulsa. (See map 1.)

Believing that the armed Blacks had instigated the firefight, Tulsa authorities joined forces with the enraged white civilians who had been at the courthouse, and together they set out to put down the "negro uprising."[8] Tulsa police haphazardly appointed between 250 and 500 white men (and even white youth) as "special deputies," granting them the authority to arrest as well as shoot and kill Black people whom they viewed as in rebellion against white Tulsans.[9] According to one eyewitness and participant in the massacre, the deputized whites were specifically told to "get a gun and get a nigger."[10] When a group of Black men gathered north of the Frisco tracks, forming a defensive wall to prevent the swelling white mob from crossing en masse into Black Tulsa, they were violently confronted around midnight by the Tulsa police, the local unit of the Oklahoma National Guard, and the hastily assembled contingent of armed "deputies."[11] (See map 1.) Whites who had already made it into the Black community were now shooting randomly through windows and setting homes and businesses on fire. In at least a few cases, Blacks were deliberately murdered, including an elderly couple who were gunned down inside their home. The most destructive and perhaps deadliest race massacre in American history had begun, and it would continue unabated for approximately twelve hours. By noon on June 1, by one contemporaneous estimate, as many as three hundred people had been killed, and Greenwood's business district, as well as more than one thousand Black residences, lay in ashes.[12]

The vast majority of contemporaneous press coverage, official reports, and subsequent histories refer to the events of May 31 and June 1, 1921, as the "Tulsa Race Riot." To be sure, since the middle of the nineteenth century, "race riot" has been the generic term used to describe outbreaks of violence between different racial or ethnic groups.[13] In the past five years, however, there has been a growing consensus within the news media and the general public around "race massacre" as the more appropriate descriptor, which is part of a larger effort to tell the story of what occurred from the vantage point of the Black victims and survivors.[14] The Tulsa Race Massacre Centennial Commission (2015–present), headed by Oklahoma state senator Kevin Matthews, is to be applauded for its leadership in initiating the conversation about how the events can be most accurately framed.[15] I believe the shift in terminology from "race riot" to "race massacre" is a necessary and timely corrective.

First and foremost, the word "massacre" better captures what actually occurred. Had the Black community been able to keep the white invaders from entering the Greenwood District, or had the violence subsided that same night, the term "riot" might be more apt. The following morning, however, white civilians and authorities banded together to launch a systematic assault on Black people and property, and that coordinated incursion places the subsequent events squarely in the realm of a massacre.

According to testimony from both Black and white eyewitnesses, by daybreak on June 1, several thousand armed whites had amassed in various locations along the southern border of the Greenwood District.[16] (See map 1.) At approximately 5:00 A.M., a whistle or siren was sounded as a signal for the invasion to begin. As the white mob stormed into Greenwood, a machine gun that had been set up atop a grain elevator sprayed bullets into Black homes, businesses, and churches along Greenwood Avenue. Airplanes flew overhead, from which whites reportedly fired pistols and shotguns (and even dropped rudimentary explosives) down at Blacks fleeing the violence.[17] The machine gun fire coupled with the air assault was a calculated ploy to facilitate the entry of the white mob and flush out any armed Black men who might have barricaded themselves in various strongholds throughout the district.

Once in Greenwood, the invading whites, civilians as well as authorities, reportedly shot and killed any Black person who was found to be armed or who did not immediately surrender, including some who were simply attempting to flee from the violence.[18] Faced with this overwhelming show of force, Black Tulsans reluctantly emerged from their homes, surrendered whatever weapons they possessed, and were taken into custody. They were transported to temporary detention centers—at Convention Hall until it was full, and then to McNulty Park and the fairgrounds—where they were held until they were able to get a white person to vouch for them.[19] There is no evidence that any of the whites involved in the mob violence were detained by authorities, let alone arrested.

Some buildings in Greenwood had already been set ablaze during the nighttime fighting, but whites now systematically looted homes, churches, and businesses and then set them on fire.[20] After some twelve hours of continuous mob violence, almost every significant structure within the thirty-five-block area had been burned to the ground or severely damaged. The invasion of the Greenwood District, in other words, was a far cry from a "race riot" or merely an outbreak of violence between two different racial or ethnic groups: it was an intentional military-style assault on a civilian community.

The financial losses were staggering, totaling approximately $2 million ($26 million in today's dollars) of Black wealth.[21] White-owned stores that had been looted by whites seeking guns and ammunition during the massacre later received restitution, but even though insurance companies and the city of Tulsa initially promised to recompense Black business owners and Black residents who had lost everything, they never made good on such reparations.[22] Furthermore, Tulsa-area banks and lending institutions refused to provide loans to Black businesses and homeowners seeking to rebuild.[23] To add insult to injury, in the days following the massacre, the city of Tulsa passed an ordinance stipulating that a home that had been destroyed by fire could be rebuilt only if it was a two-story structure, and only on condition that fire-retardant materials were utilized in the construction. This measure would have made it impossible for most, if not all, Black business owners and

Black residents to rebuild. Fortunately, the local district court (perhaps in conjunction with the Oklahoma Supreme Court) issued a permanent injunction against the fire ordinance.[24] Nonetheless, Tulsa city leaders had made manifest their intentions to prevent the rebuilding of the Greenwood District. In retrospect, the actions of the white mob and local authorities can only be interpreted as a concerted attempt to expel Tulsa's Black community, as had happened elsewhere in the region.[25] Seemingly underlining this point, a photo of Greenwood engulfed in heavy smoke is captioned "Runing [*sic*] the Negro out of Tulsa" (fig. 1.17).

Despite the best efforts of the white mob and the city's leaders, Black Tulsans rebuilt the Greenwood District brick by brick. By 1942, according to attorney and historian Hannibal Johnson, the district had reached its zenith, with more than 242 Black-owned and Black-operated businesses.[26] In the final analysis, an important legacy of the Tulsa Race Massacre has proven to be the grit and resilience of the Black survivors.

PHOTOGRAPHING A MASSACRE

Not only is the 1921 Tulsa Race Massacre the most destructive episode of anti-Black violence in American history, but it is likely one of the most photographed episodes as well. In conducting the research for this book, I reviewed more than five hundred photos of the massacre.[27] To my knowledge, similar outbreaks of anti-Black violence in Chicago (1919), Elaine, Arkansas (1919), and Rosewood, Florida (1923), did not produce an equivalent number of photos. Not only does the large cache of extant photographs afford us an opportunity to understand the depth and ferocity of anti-Black violence during the post–World War I era, but the images also provide an unvarnished glimpse into the psychological underpinnings of white supremacist violence, revealing the documentary choices that white participants made as the massacre unfolded. Moreover, the sheer number of these photos is illustrative of how photographing brutal acts of anti-Black violence had become an important social ritual in early-twentieth-century America. Because so many photos of the race massacre are still available to us today, we are compelled, even obliged, to engage with them. In reckoning with this pictorial legacy, there are some questions we must ask ourselves: Why do so many photos exist? Who took them? What do they tell us about the events they depict? In addressing these questions with sensitivity and empathy, I hope that I can use the photos to shed greater light on aspects of the race massacre that might be faint or imperceptible in other documentary sources.

The photographs contained in this volume do not and were not meant to provide a balanced or objective view of events. They do not depict the events that led to the armed invasion of Greenwood; nor do they show white mob participants engaged in the violent destruction. If such photos ever existed, they remain hidden away in private collections or have been destroyed over time. Rather, the available photos primarily depict the aftermath of the white rampage on the morning of June 1. The bulk of the photos I analyzed show burned-out Greenwood homes and businesses along with armed white men rounding up the district's Black community. Moreover, they frame what occurred almost exclusively from white Tulsans' perspective. Of the more than five hundred photographs I reviewed, only the half-dozen images by photographer Reverend Jacob H. Hooker, himself a survivor of the massacre, are attributed to a Black person. Reverend Hooker's photos poignantly capture the destruction and rebuilding of Greenwood. (See figs. 1.28, 4.10, 4.16, and 4.17.) Unfortunately, his photography studio, located at 22 North Elgin Avenue, was burned down during the massacre and was never rebuilt.

In addition, I have included a group of photos that depict American Red Cross workers attending to Blacks injured and displaced in the massacre, as well as assisting with the subsequent reconstruction. For more than six months, through December 1921, the Red Cross oversaw emergency relief efforts in the community. Maurice Willows, who directed the organization's operations in Tulsa, was described by Black survivors as an "angel of mercy" who selflessly assisted destitute Greenwood residents in their time of greatest need. For that reason, photos taken by photographer Gifford I. Talmage on behalf of the Red Cross are prominently featured in this book.

An extensive race massacre photo archive exists because so many white participants desired to visually represent and share with other whites their role in the violent destruction of the Greenwood District. White Tulsans' eagerness to photograph the community's devastation was reflective of turn-of-the century lynching culture, in which photography was central. By and large, lynching culture revolved around white mobs torturing and summarily killing Black people in public. White-on-Black lynching often became a public spectacle, with as many as several thousand people in attendance. White mobs sought to portray the white community as undifferentiated and united in enacting white supremacy through terroristic violence enacted upon Black bodies. For example, photo postcards of lynchings often pictured a crowd of gleeful whites posing near a lynched Black body.[28] According to historian Amy Wood, there was an appetite among white Americans for witnessing a lynching because it gave them social authority in telling the story as well as the ability to frame themselves as protectors of the community.[29]

The white Tulsans who invaded Greenwood similarly portrayed themselves as protectors, defending their community against an armed "negro uprising." Through taking or sharing photos of destroyed Greenwood buildings and, especially, of armed whites escorting Black men with their hands raised in surrender, white participants and onlookers sought to demonstrate that white Tulsans had succeeded in thwarting Black violence. Captions such as "Running the Negro out of Tulsa," "Little Africa on Fire" (fig. 1.21), and "Herding Them in the Convention Hall" are indicative of this cultural ethos.[30] Race massacre photos were valued as souvenirs that enabled their authors to credibly inscribe themselves into a triumphalist narrative.[31] This is particularly true of those later sold as photo postcards, which also allowed those who purchased and sent them, as well as the recipients who then viewed them, to vicariously share in that triumph.

Although white mob participants enthusiastically took pictures of Greenwood's destruction, most did not leave a documentary record that would later allow their photos to be traced back to them. This was not an uncommon dynamic. As with lynching photography, rarely did white photographers or whites pictured in race massacre photos identify themselves. The bulk of the images for which a specific creator can be identified were taken by amateur white male photographers. For example, Francis Albert Schmidt, who was the University of Tulsa's football coach at the time, and University of Tulsa alumnus Joseph McMinn Hause are known to have taken some of the photos that document the detention of Black Tulsans at Convention Hall and McNulty Park.[32] In contrast to others' wide-angle images, Schmidt's and Hause's photos provide close-up views of Black families being searched by deputized whites and then loaded onto waiting trucks. (See figs. 2.4–2.10 and 2.12–2.13.) In addition, there are approximately a half-dozen extant photos by Schmidt of the corpses of Black massacre victims. Like his detention images, these photos were taken at close range, revealing victims' facial expressions, wounds, and personal effects. (See figs. 1.9–1.11 and 1.13.) As many as three hundred people are estimated to have died as a result of the massacre, and yet it is rare to find photos that provide visual evidence of the fatalities.

It is unlikely that Schmidt's and Hause's photos were intended to document the Black experience of the race massacre; nevertheless, they bring into stark focus the horrific violence suffered by Tulsa's Black community. At the time, only the state's Black newspapers (particularly Oklahoma City's *Black Dispatch*) and nationally distributed Black newspapers such as the *Chicago Defender* carried stories on the massacre from the vantage point of Black victims and survivors, under headlines such as "Loot, Murder, Arson! Four Million Dollars Lost," "Tulsa Aflame; 85 Dead in Riot," and "Police Aided Tulsa Rioters."[33] Rather than send reporters and photographers to Tulsa to cover the massacre directly, the editors repurposed photos circulating in white dailies to illustrate how white mob violence coupled with the complicity of city officials led to high Black fatalities and to Greenwood's physical destruction. Black newspapers' critical approach to utilizing white-authored race massacre photos to tell the story of Black massacre victims and survivors is in many ways the template upon which this photographic history is based.

Some of the most memorable photos of the massacre were taken not by amateurs but by two of Tulsa's most established professional photographers, Clarence Jack and Alvin Krupnick. In addition to owning his own studio, Jack was a staff photographer for the *Tulsa World*. He was widely respected for his panoramic images, which were often lauded in the pages of the paper itself.[34] During this period, he and Krupnick frequently ran advertisements in the *World* to promote their respective photography businesses. Krupnick was not beyond a bit of brash self-promotion. "When you think of Kodaks think of Alvin Krupnick," he encouraged would-be customers in one of his ads.[35] In another he reprinted a letter he had received from a customer praising his photo development. "Dear Sir: The developing and printing . . . was the best I have ever had," the writer stated. "I showed the pictures to some friends here [St. Louis, Missouri] and they are going to send you all their kodak work hereafter."[36] Jack and Krupnick brought the skill and attentiveness for which they were known to the photos they took of the race massacre. In fact, Krupnick is credited for many of the photos in the National Association for the Advancement of Colored People's frequently cited race massacre photo collection.[37]

One might expect that, as the *Tulsa World's* primary staff photographer, Jack would have contributed extensively to the newspaper's race massacre coverage. Yet it appears that in the first two weeks of coverage, the paper printed only a handful of race massacre photos, and none of them were attributed to Jack. In comparison, the *World's* chief competitor, the *Tulsa Tribune*, published the "first photo" of the massacre on June 1, followed by several more photos over the next week.[38] The conspicuous absence of images by Jack is all the more confounding given that he took several high-quality wide-angle photos of Greenwood landmarks that were destroyed during the mob violence. (See figs. 1.32–1.34.) Interestingly, at least three uncredited photos taken by Krupnick accompanied the *Tulsa World's* June 2nd coverage.[39] A week following the massacre, one of Krupnick's most compelling images was published in the *New York Times* (fig. 2.14).[40] Depicting a dejected Black female survivor sitting on the back of a truck with her few salvaged possessions, exhaustion and desperation clearly etched on her face, it evocatively captured the human tragedy of the massacre. In the days and months ahead, Krupnick would continue to photograph the Greenwood District and its Black survivors. His post-massacre photos document Greenwood's gradual reemergence from rubble-filled ruins, to a tent city, to restored homes and businesses (figs. 5.10–5.11). Krupnick's race massacre photography is both eloquent and historically important, but there is another point that should not be overlooked: as the owner of a commercial studio, he likely processed numerous photos for white customers who had taken part in the massacre. Without the presence of professional photographers like Alvin Krupnick and Clarence Jack, there would not be as many high-quality photos to help tell the story of what happened.

It has long been rumored that Tulsa police were sent to photography studios throughout the city to confiscate any massacre photos that were being developed. While this rumor has never been either disputed or confirmed by archival research, a box containing confiscated photos allegedly surfaced at the Tulsa police station more than fifty years later, in 1972 or 1973. A sergeant purportedly showed the photos to several officers in a break room. Thirty years later, one of the officers who had seen the confiscated photos shared the story with archivist and local historian Dick Warner. He told Warner that the photos he viewed were gruesome. One he remembered showed the lifeless bodies of a Black man, a Black woman, and two children draped over a fence. In another, a Black man was being dragged behind a car. Several of the photos, he believed, showed white men digging trenches in which the bodies of Black massacre victims were being dumped. After this brief reemergence, the confiscated photos seemingly disappeared again; and despite the efforts of historians Dick Warner and Scott Ellsworth to locate them, they have not been found. With the current efforts to locate a mass grave at Tulsa's Oaklawn Cemetery and other sites, we may hope to soon know whether there is any validity to the stories associated with the long-lost photos.[41]

While some undoubtedly would rather not acknowledge this episode in Oklahoma's history, what happened in Tulsa during those two days in 1921 must never be forgotten. As the images in this book make clear, it is essential that we choose to remember the race massacre. And it is essential that we do so in ways that center the victims and survivors.

PURPOSE AND RATIONALE

As a historian of lynching and racial violence, I have spent nearly my entire career studying the ways in which Black people and Black communities have experienced, made sense of, and ultimately resisted white terrorist violence. The 1921 Tulsa Race Massacre has been a staple of my teaching. I have often discussed the events against the backdrop of the numerous white mob attacks on Black communities during the Red Summer of 1919 as well as the post–World War 1 lynching of returning Black soldiers. In many ways, I thought I understood the race massacre. However, it was not until I moved to Oklahoma in 2016 and began teaching at the University of Oklahoma that I fully began to appreciate the scope and gravity of those fateful twelve hours in Tulsa.

My interactions with the community transformed both my understanding of this history and the way I relate to it. Not long after I arrived in Oklahoma, I made several trips to Tulsa to visit the Greenwood Cultural Center and the John Hope Franklin Center for Reconciliation, the city's primary Black cultural heritage organizations. I was pleasantly struck by the prominence these anchor institutions accorded to the history of Black Wall Street and the race massacre within the Greenwood community. Eighty historical markers indicate the former locations of Black businesses along Greenwood Avenue (the district's main thoroughfare historically and contemporarily), Archer Street, Cameron Street, and Cincinnati Avenue. (See map 1A.) A giant mural devoted to the memory of Black Wall Street is emblazoned on the interstate overpass that bisects Greenwood Avenue. And even a casual passerby could not help but notice and be drawn to Reconciliation Park, which commemorates the legacy of the race massacre through public art. As a historian of racial violence, I know that most communities are unaware of their own history of anti-Black violence, and few of those that are aware choose to draw attention to it with historical markers.[42]

It was the foregrounding of the race massacre in Greenwood that inspired my deep desire to write a book that would highlight the perspectives of the Black survivors. The voices of Black victims of white supremacist violence are typically absent from public history and official narratives. Despite the long history of Black lynching in the United States, for example, only recently has there been a significant memorial dedicated to its victims.[43] During the trial that was hastily convened in Tulsa in the days following the race massacre, the two groups of Black men who had gone to the courthouse to offer protection to Dick Rowland were blamed for instigating the violence that erupted.[44] (Ironically, the claim that Dick Rowland attacked Sarah Page was never substantiated, and the charges against him were subsequently dismissed.)[45] The belief that "riotous" Black Tulsans provoked the massacre provided white Tulsans with a convenient justification for their wanton violence. The assertion that it was a "negro uprising" has reverberated through time and remains one of the most egregious misrepresentations of the massacre—especially when we consider that neither the city of Tulsa nor any white person involved in the violence has ever been held accountable for their actions.[46]

It took eighty years and the extensive research conducted in 1997–2001 by the Tulsa Race Riot Commission to document and discredit the idea that Black Tulsans were to blame for the violence.[47] While the commission's groundbreaking investigation and analysis has provided a solid foundation for understanding what occurred, the work of recovering, highlighting, and validating the experiences of the victims and survivors is ongoing. In both small and large ways, I hope this book will shed light on what Black Tulsans experienced in one of the worst episodes of anti-Black violence in American history, and what they had to overcome in its aftermath. One of my chief aims in undertaking this project was to honor those whose lives were lost or forever changed through telling the story of the race massacre from their perspectives and on their terms.

While the history of Black Wall Street and the race massacre is at the forefront of Greenwood's community conscience, it is faint and in some cases nonexistent in other communities across Oklahoma. Many of the students who enroll in my history of lynching course— most of whom are from Oklahoma—have only vaguely heard about the

Greenwood District and the violence that was unleashed upon the community that night. In order to explain their lack of knowledge, they often claim that the race massacre was barely touched upon or was not even discussed in their high school Oklahoma history course. Not completely satisfied with this answer, I vowed to talk with middle and high school social studies teachers about their approach to teaching the massacre. As I dug further, my students' recollections were confirmed. Many of the teachers I spoke with revealed that while the race massacre is historicallyimportant, they did not feel that they had the proper grounding or resources to do justice to the topic. Whereas the Greenwood District's efforts to keep this history alive inspired me to share the community's story, my encounters with Oklahoma teachers and students cemented my commitment to creating broader opportunities for teachers to engage in dialogues about Oklahoma Black history. Thus, this book is both an outgrowth of and a response to how I have experienced the history of the massacre during my time in Oklahoma.

In the past two decades, several important books on the Tulsa Race Massacre have refined our knowledge of what occurred.[48] Most recently, Randy Krehbiel's *Tulsa, 1921: Reporting a Massacre* (2019) has highlighted the active role that Tulsa-area white newspapers played in setting the stage for the white mob's rampage through Greenwood. By presenting in one volume the most compelling available images, those that best represent the Black experience of the race massacre, this book will build upon and reinforce the new literature. Even though the vast majority of the photos were taken by whites, they nonetheless show what happened to Greenwood and the Black residents who lived there.

THIS PHOTOGRAPHIC HISTORY IS ORGANIZED chronologically and divided into six thematic chapters. Chapter 1, "The Massacre," presents photos of whites who participated in the massacre, photos of Black victims of white mob violence, and photos that highlight the destruction to homes, businesses, and churches within the Greenwood District. The photos in chapter 2, "Internment," show Black Tulsans being forcibly taken to detention centers throughout the city. Chapter 3, "Angels of Mercy," focuses on the Red Cross workers who provided emergency assistance to Black Tulsans who were injured or displaced as a result of the violence. Chapter 4, "Refugees," consists primarily of photos of Black survivors who were forced to live in tents and makeshift structures after their homes were destroyed. Black children who lost parents are also a focal point. Chapter 5, "Rebuilding and Renaissance," showcases the efforts of Black Tulsans to rebuild their homes, churches, and businesses in the months following the race massacre. The chapter culminates with photos of the Greenwood District post-1921, when the community was thriving again. Chapter 6, "Remembering the Survivors," contains photos of forty-one Black Tulsans who lived through the violence, along with some personal remembrances. A brief epilogue then comments on the need to confront the photographic legacies of the massacre.

The more than 150 photos herein were selected because of their historic value and their evocative power. Within the chapters they are interspersed with reminiscences by Black survivors, who thus serve as the chief narrators of the events depicted. While I consulted a variety of primary and secondary sources for these reminiscences, I primarily utilize two collections of Black survivor accounts. First and foremost is Mary Parrish's *Events of the Tulsa Disaster* (1923), a gem of a historical document that authentically captures Black Tulsans' anger, disillusionment, and resilience following the massacre.[49] Most notably, the book contains accounts by survivors who painfully recall dodging machine gun fire and airplanes dropping explosives on Greenwood, as well as Parrish's own dramatic description of how she and her daughter escaped from Greenwood as it was being overrun by the white mob. In order to bolster her recounting of events, Parrish solicited testimonials from fifteen Black survivors. These statements were composed within two or three weeks of the massacre and therefore contain vivid details that oral history interviews conducted long after an event typically lack. Because of the level of detail in Parrish's and these survivors' descriptions of the massacre, I quote from them extensively.

I also draw at length on the Tulsa Race Riot Commission's oral history collection *Tulsa Race Riot Survivors' Stories*, an invaluable resource for understanding Black shared memory of the massacre.[50] Between 1997 and 2001, the commission tracked down and registered approximately 120 race massacre survivors. Of the 120 identified, approximately half were interviewed by the commission. The living survivors ranged in age from 74 to 103. Half of them were in the Tulsa area, and the remainder were in various locales across the United States. With only two known race massacre survivors living as of 2020, *Survivors' Stories*, the largest compilation of survivor accounts, constitutes a priceless documentary record of the Black experience of the race massacre.

My ultimate goal with this book is to pay tribute to the victims and survivors of the Tulsa Race Massacre. I hope that readers will join me in honoring their tremendous sacrifice and resilience.

1. Larry O'Dell, "Riot Property Loss," in Oklahoma Commission to Study the Tulsa Race Riot of 1921, *Tulsa Race Riot: A Report* (Oklahoma City, 2001), p. 144.

2. Ibid., 149.

3. Profiles of Greenwood's most notable residents can be found in Johnson, *Black Wall Street*, chap. 1.

4. Scott Ellsworth, *Death in a Promised Land: The Tulsa Race Riot* (Baton Rouge: Louisiana State University Press, 1992), 44–47; Randy Kreibel, *Tulsa, 1921: Reporting a Massacre* (Norman: University of Oklahoma Press, 2019), 35–36.

5. Kreibel, *Tulsa, 1921*, 36–37.

6. See Jacqueline Dowd Hall, "'The Mind That Burns in Each Body': Women, Rape, and Racial Violence," Southern Exposure 12 (1984): 61–71; For three excellent treatments of lynching and the "protection of womanhood" discourse, see Hall, *Revolt against Chivalry: Jessie Daniel Ames and the Women's Campaign against Lynching* (New York: Columbia University Press, 1993); Crystal N. Feimster, *Southern Horrors: Women and the Politics of Rape and Lynching* (Cambridge, MA: Harvard University Press, 2009); and Estelle B. Freedman, *Redefining Rape: Sexual Violence in the Era of Suffrage and Segregation* (Cambridge, MA: Harvard University Press, 2013).

7. Krehbiel, *Tulsa, 1921*, p. 43.

8. Ibid., pp. 43–46; Scott Ellsworth, "The Tulsa Race Riot" in Oklahoma Commission, *Tulsa Race Riot*, p. 63.

9. Ellsworth, "Tulsa Race Riot," p. 64.

10. Ibid.

11. Alfred Brophy, *Reconstructing the Dreamland: The Tulsa Riot of 1921; Race, Reparations, and Reconciliation* (New York: Oxford University Press, 2002), pp. 58–59.

12. In his narrative report, dated December 31, 1921, Disaster Relief Director Maurice Willows asserted that estimates for the number killed ranged from fifty-five to as many as three hundred. Due to hasty burials and the lack of recordkeeping, he acknowledged that an accurate accounting of the number of people killed during the race massacre was impossible. Willows's narrative report is reprinted in Johnson, *Black Wall Street*, pp. 200–216. A scanned copy can be consulted at https://www.tulsahistory.org/wp-content/uploads/2018/11/1921-Red-Cross-Report-December-30th.pdf.

13. See Bernard F. Robinson, "The Sociology of Race Riots," *Phylon* 2, no. 2 (1941): 162–171; Linda K. Kerber, "Abolitionists and Amalgamators: The New York City Race Riots of 1834," *New York History* 48, no. 1 (1967): 28–39; John M. Werner, *Reaping the Bloody Harvest: Race Riots in the United States during the Age of Jackson, 1824–1849* (New York: Garland, 1986); Dominic J. Capeci Jr., "Foreword: American Race Rioting in Historical Perspective," in Walter Rucker and James Nathaniel Upton, eds., *Encyclopedia of American Race Riots*, 2 vols. (Westport, CT: Greenwood Press, 2007), vol. 1, pp. xix–xlii; and "Introduction," ibid., pp. xlv–liii. See also David Grimsted, *American Mobbing, 1828–1861: Toward Civil War* (New York: Oxford University Press, 1998).

14. Samuel Hardiman, "'Race Riot Is a Euphemism': Teachers Learn Why Tulsa Race Massacre Is More Accurate Term," *Tulsa World*, June 12, 2018, https://www.tulsaworld.com/news/local/education/race-riot-is-a-euphemism-teachers-learn-why-tulsa-race/article_37e95c53-9f55-5ba8-8ffa-c5586946a420.html; "Tulsa Race Massacre," History.com, March 8, 2018, updated October 21, 2019, https://www.history.com/topics/roaring-twenties/tulsa-race-massacre; "Tulsa Race Massacre," in *The Encyclopedia of Oklahoma History and Culture* (online), https://www.okhistory.org/publications/enc/entry.php?entry=TU013; "1921 Tulsa Race Massacre" (online exhibit), Tulsa Historical Society and Museum, https://www.tulsahistory.org/exhibit/1921-tulsa-race-massacre/.

15. Randy Krehbiel, "Tulsa Race Riot Centennial Commission Announced," *Tulsa World*, February 25, 2017, https://www.tulsaworld.com/news/local/government-and-politics/tulsa-race-riot-centennial-commission-announced/article_0d2b43c2-1ef4-59f3-a21ad9c0a6b90d8a.html. See also the commission's website, https://www.tulsa2021.org.

16. Brophy, *Reconstructing the Dreamland*, pp. 62–63; Krehbiel, *Tulsa, 1921*, p. 71

17. For documentation and a careful analysis of the use of airplanes in the assault on Greenwood, see Richard S. Warner, "Airplanes and the Riot," in Oklahoma Commission, *Tulsa Race Riot*, pp. 103–108.

18. Ellsworth, "Tulsa Race Riot," pp. 74–79.

19. Ellsworth, *Death in a Promised Land*, pp. 71–72.

20. Ellsworth, "Tulsa Race Riot," pp. 74–79.

21. O'Dell, "Riot Property Loss," p. 149.

22. Ibid., p. 145.

23. Johnson, *Black Wall Street*, p. 99.

24. Ellsworth, *Death in a Promised Land*, pp. 84–89.

25. See Kimberly Harper, *White Man's Heaven: The Lynching and Expulsion of Blacks in the Southern Ozarks, 1894–1909* (Fayetteville: University of Arkansas Press, 2012). See also Guy Lancaster, "'They Are Not Wanted': The Extirpation of African Americans from Baxter County, Arkansas," *Arkansas Historical Quarterly* 69, no. 1 (2010): 28–43; Lancaster, "Nightriding and Racial Cleansing in the Arkansas River Valley," *Arkansas Historical Quarterly* 72, no. 3 (2013): 242–264; and Lancaster, "'There Are Not Many Colored People Here:' African Americans in Polk County, Arkansas, 1896–1937," 70, no. 4 (2011): 429–449.

26. Johnson, *Black Wall Street*, p. 116.

27. The most significant collections of photos were donated to the Oklahoma Historical Society, the Tulsa Historical Society, the University of Tulsa, the Library of Congress, the University of Oklahoma, and Northeastern Oklahoma State University.

28. For a photographic example of a spectacle lynching along with an extended discussion of lynching culture, see Karlos K. Hill, *Beyond the Rope: The Impact of Lynching on Black Culture and Memory* (New York: Cambridge University Press, 2016), pp. 2–3, chaps. 2–3.

29. For a more detailed discussion of spectacle lynchings as representative of white supremacy, see Amy L. Wood, *Lynching and Spectacle: Witnessing Racial Violence in America, 1890–1940* (Chapel Hill: University of North Carolina Press, 2009), pp. 87–92.

30. For "Herding Them in the Convention Hall," see Tulsa Race Massacre Collection, Tulsa Historical Society and Museum, catalog number 2018.118.009.

31. Of the five hundred race massacre photos I analyzed, approximately two dozen had been transformed into photo postcards and subsequently sold commercially.

32. Carlson, "Tulsa Race Massacre." In addition to Schmidt and Hause, this volume includes race massacre photos by amateur photographers Charles L. Reeder and Arthur Dudley. For biographical information on known race massacre photographers, see I. Marc Carlson, "Tulsa Race Riot Photographers," http://www.personal.utulsa.edu/~marc-carlson/riot/photographers.htm. See also Carlson, "Known Race Riot Photographers," The Tulsa Race Massacre, https://tulsaraceriot.wordpress.com/research-topics/known-race-riot-photographers/.

33. For examples of Black newspaper coverage of the race massacre, see *Black Dispatch*, June 11, October 22, and December 8, 1921; and *Chicago Defender*, June 4, June 11, and June 18, 1921.

34. For examples of the *Tulsa World*'s praise of Jack's photography, see "The New Business Sky Line of Tulsa From Catholic Church," *Tulsa Daily World*, September 10, 1916, 1, cols. 2–4, https://gateway.okhistory.org/ark:/67531/metadc134140/?q=%22clarence%20jack%22; and *Tulsa Daily World*, October 30, 1916, 1, col. 1 (bottom), https://gateway.okhistory.org/ark:/67531/metadc134186/?q=%22clarence%20jack%22.

35. "When You Think of Kodaks Think of Alvin Krupnick" (ad), *Tulsa Daily World*, September 23, 1919, 2, col. 2, https://gateway.okhistory.org/ark:/67531/metadc146165/?q=%22alvin%20krupnick%22.

36. "I Am Rather Proud of This Letter" (ad), *Tulsa Daily World*, May 23, 1919, 6, cols. 4–5, https://gateway.okhistory.org/ark:/67531/metadc136087/?q=%22alvin%20krupnick%22.

37. For more information on and access to this collection, see Alvin C. Krupnick Co., photographer, NAACP Photographs of Race Riots in Columbia, Tenn., Los Angeles, Calif., and Tulsa, Okla., Library of Congress, https://www.loc.gov/item/95516152/.

38. For a brief description and compilation of published *Tulsa Tribune* and *Tulsa World* photos of the massacre, see I. Marc Carlson's website *Tulsa Race Riot Photographs*, https://tulsaraceriot.omeka.net/collections/.

39. "In the Wake of Tulsa's Race War," *Tulsa Daily World*, June 2, 1921, p. 1, col. 4. Last accessed April 1, 2020. https://gateway.okhistory.org/ark:/67531/metadc77783/?q=tulsa%20daily%20world%20june%202%2C%201921.

40. See *New York Times*, June 8, 1921, 1, col. 1. For information regarding the city of Tulsa's investigation into mass graves, see Mihir Zaveri, "Nearly 100 Years after Tulsa Massacre, City Plans to Search Cemetery for Victims," *New York Times*, February 5, 2020, https://www.nytimes.com/2020/02/05/us/tulsa-race-massacre-mass-grave.html; Kurtis Lee, "Tulsa Finally Decides to Address 1921 Race Massacre with Search for Mass Grave," *Los Angeles Times*, February 4, 2020, https://www.latimes.com/world-nation/story/2020-02-04/tulsa-set-to-excavate-bodies-from; and Nehemiah D. Frank, "Researchers Have Found Evidence of Mass Graves from the 1921 Tulsa Race Massacre. Here's Why That News Is Bittersweet for My Community," *Time*, December 18, 2019, https://time.com/5752347/tulsa-mass-graves-race-massacre/.

41. Information regarding the rumored Tulsa police confiscation of race massacre photos and he subsequent cover-up is outlined in a memo from Dick Warner to Scott Ellsworth dated June 12, 2002. The memo is in this author's possession.

42. Brentin Mock, "Why Memorializing America's History of Racism Matters," *CityLab*, July 6, 2015, https://www.citylab.com/design/2015/07/why-memorializing-americas-history-of-racism-matters/397781/; "EJI's Lynching Marker Project Grows," Equal Justice Initiative, September 12, 2016, https://eji.org/news/eji-lynching-marker-project-grows/.

43. Equal Justice Initiative, "Memorial" (last accessed February 4, 2020), https://museumandmemorial.eji.org/memorial.

44. Ellsworth, "Tulsa Race Riot," p. 89.

45. Ibid.

46. Alfred L. Brophy, "Assessing State and City Culpability: The Riot and the Law," in Oklahoma Commission, *Tulsa Race Riot*, p. 167.

47. Ibid.

48. For an excellent review of past and recent scholarship on the race massacre, see Joshua D. Mackey, "Breaking a Century of Silence: A Historiography of the Tulsa Race Riot," *Fairmount Folio* 19 (2019): 49–61, https://journals.wichita.edu/index.php/ff/article/view/228.

49. Mary E. Jones Parrish, *Events of the Tulsa Disaster: An Eye-Witness Account of the 1921 Tulsa Race Riot* (1923; facsimile ed., Tulsa, OK: John Hope Franklin Center for Reconciliation, 2016).

50. Survivors' Stories, box 12, folders 9–12, Tulsa Race Riot Commission Materials, 1921–1923/1997–2001, Oklahoma Historical Society. The videotaped accounts were transcribed and submitted as hard copy to the Oklahoma Legislative Commission to Study the Tulsa Race Riot.

The Greenwood District
before the Race Massacre

Vernon African Methodist Episcopal Church, 311 North Greenwood Avenue, circa 1914. Vernon A.M.E. may have been the first church established in the Greenwood District.

FIGURE 0.2
Tulsa Historical Society and Museum
Beryl D. Ford Collection

Looking north on Greenwood Avenue
from Archer Street, circa 1918. The inter-
section, a block north of the Saint Louis–
San Francisco ("Frisco") Railway tracks,
marked the start of the Greenwood
District and served as a border between
white Tulsa and Black Tulsa.

FIGURE 0.3
Tulsa Historical Society and Museum

An angled view of Greenwood and Archer circa 1920. An array of Black-owned businesses dotted the first two blocks of Greenwood north of Archer, a stretch that was known as "Deep Greenwood."

FIGURE 0.4
Tulsa Historical Society and Museum

The home of Greenwood residents Samuel and Lucy Mackey at 418 North Greenwood Avenue, circa 1921. Lucy Mackey was a domestic worker, and Samuel Mackey was a porter and may have owned a modest real estate business. As a Black working-class family, the Mackeys were able to accrue wealth and build a home that was comparable to residences in Tulsa's elite white neighborhoods.

FIGURE 0.5
Tulsa Historical Society and Museum
Beryl D. Ford Collection

Booker T. Washington High School, on
East Easton Street between Frankfort
Avenue and Elgin Place, circa 1921.
Erected in 1913, the school was one of the
few structures that were not damaged
or destroyed during the race massacre. It
subsequently served as the headquarters
for the American Red Cross relief effort.

FIGURE 0.6
Greenwood Cultural Center

The Williams Dreamland Theatre, 127 North Greenwood Avenue, circa 1921. Opened in 1914, the Dreamland hosted silent films, music concerts, and lectures. As the first Black movie theater in Tulsa as well as the first Black entertainment space in the state of Oklahoma, it was an important symbol of Black Wall Street's affluence prior to the race massacre.

FIGURE 0.7
Tulsa Historical Society and Museum

John Wesley Williams, his wife, Loula Cotton Williams, and their son W. D. Williams out for a drive in their automobile. John was an engineer for the Thompson Ice Cream Company, and Loula was a schoolteacher. The Williamses owned the Dreamland Theatre. They were the first Black family in Tulsa to own a car.

1

The Massacre

The evening before the Tulsa Race Riot of 1921 began, my husband, Thomas, and I went to church, to Paradise Baptist Church just off of Greenwood Avenue. The churches used to hold BTU meetings Sunday nights. They done quit holdin' them now. Thomas got up and told the congregation about a vision he had.

He said, "I don't know what it's going to be, but it's going to be some kind of destruction." Several of the church people questioned him about whether the message had really come from God, or from Thomas. My husband kept explainin' his vision and most of the people believed him. Some of them, though, made light of him. He just said to them, "We'll see."

When we got out of BTU that night, he went on home to our little house at 519 West Latimer Street. Thomas didn't say no more about his vision. I went to bed, but he was still up. A little after midnight, he woke me up and said, "Wife, it's time for us to go!" I said, "Go where?" He said, "I told you something was goin' to happen; well it's happening now. A man just run by the house and he said 'Brothers, get your guns, get your guns, a riot has broke out.'"

ROSA DAVIS SKINNER

interviewed in 1994
North Tulsa Oral History Project, transcript, p. 127

The first information that I received of the Riot came about 9:20 o'clock Tuesday night, May 31st, 1921. I was attending a play given by the Senior Class. A little boy came up, almost out of breath, and exclaimed, "They are trying to lynch a Colored man down town and the Colored people are going down to prevent it."

The meeting broke up in some confusion and all went home. We sat up at our house till about midnight and then we decided to go to bed. There was little sleeping, for the noise of guns kept us awake all night.

About 5 o'clock a very peculiar whistle blew. This seemed to have been a signal for a concerted attack by the whites, for immediately a terrible gun fire began. Aeroplanes also began to fly over very low; what they were doing I cannot say for I was in my room."

JAMES T. A. WEST
a high school teacher

June 20, 1921
Parrish, *Events of the Tulsa Disaster*, p. 24

FIGURE I.I
Tulsa Historical Society and Museum

During the evening of May 31 and the early morning hours of June 1, white Tulsans randomly attacked Blacks whom they encountered in downtown Tulsa. Scores—perhaps hundreds—of whites and Blacks exchanged gunfire across the Frisco Railroad tracks, where night fighting was the heaviest. Pictured here is a rare photo of a race massacre victim that was taken prior to the invasion of Greenwood on the morning of June 1.

At the section line I met Mrs. Thompson, her husband and family. They were on a truck and had started east. She called to me and I ran to them and got on the truck. . . . After we had gone several miles we began to see automobile loads of men with guns going east ahead of us. We wondered where they were going but we were not destined to wonder long, for as we neared the aviation fields we saw their destination. The planes were out of the sheds, all in readiness for flying, and these men with highpowered rifles were getting into them. As we went further we saw several men leaving the fields, going to the house, returning with guns and heading towards Tulsa.

MARY PARRISH "My Experience in Tulsa"
Events of the Tulsa Disaster, p. 11

THE MASSACRE

FIGURE 1.2
Tulsa Historical Society and Museum
Beryl D. Ford Collection

A carload of armed white men, likely
heading toward the Greenwood District
during the race massacre. They had
probably been deputized and given orders
by Tulsa police to help quell the "negro
uprising."

Arose about 4:30 Wednesday a.m. and saw people rushing from Greenwood and that section of the town. A group of Whites, stationed on the hill, fired upon them, some falling, others struggling on to safety. Then it dawned upon me of the danger of my invalid mother who has been helpless for four years. She was about six blocks from me up in the direction from which the people were fleeing.

I reached her in the midst of a rain of bullets. My sisters and I gathered her up, placed her on a cot and three of us carried the cot and the other one carried a bundle of clothes; thus we carried mother about six blocks, with bullets falling on all sides. About six squads of rioters overtook us, asked for men and guns, made us hold up our hands. There were boys in the bunch from about 10 years upward, all armed with guns.

MRS. CARRIE KINLAW

June 23, 1921
Parrish, *Events of the Tulsa Disaster*, p. 36

THE MASSACRE

FIGURE 1.3
Tulsa Historical Society and Museum

White civilians were only too eager to take up arms and assist the authorities in "protecting" the community.

FIGURE 1.4
Tulsa Historical Society and Museum

Looting was rampant during the massacre, as the white invaders took items from homes, businesses, and churches. The man in this photo looks to be guarding his new possessions. A handwritten note on the back reads "Proud of his pilfering. Race pride far astray."

So everybody was scared you know people shooting going on. And we saw those soldiers we don't know what these soldiers was to protect or kill us.

ANNIE BEARD

interviewed April 16, 1999
Tulsa Race Riot Survivors' Stories, tape 2, p. 63

FIGURE 1.5
University of Tulsa, McFarlin Library

Black oral histories of the race massacre
are replete with recollections of machine
guns being fired at Greenwood buildings
and fleeing Blacks. One was reportedly
manned by the National Guard.

NATIONAL GUARD
MACHINE GUN CREW
DURING TULSA RACE RIOT 6-1-21

FIGURE 1.6
Tulsa Historical Society and Museum

Here the image has been cropped and
resized to create a photographic postcard,
intended to be sold as a "souvenir" of the
massacre and its aftermath.

NEGRO SLAIN IN TULSA RIOT JUNE-1-1921

FIGURE I.7
Tulsa Historical Society and Museum

Victims' corpses were a macabre subject for postcards intended to be sold commercially and sent through the mail. Although there were whites killed during the massacre, there are no extant photos, and certainly no postcards, that include views of white bodies. The white audience for whom massacre postcards were created had no desire to see photos of whites who had been killed by Blacks. Rather, the photos of victims that whites took and shared were intended to show that rebellious Blacks had been subdued.

When we left our house I was so afraid, because bullets were coming down around us, the planes were up in the air shooting down and I could hear those bullets falling. And all of a sudden when we got to the track, I went over the track and there was a lot of people running and dodging the bullets and just afraid. So I went and ran into a chicken coop.

ELDORIS McCONDICHIE

interviewed April 16, 1999
Tulsa Race Riot Survivors' Stories, tape 2, p. 67

The Frisco tracks and station form a dividing line between the business section of White Tulsa and Black Tulsa. It was here that the first battle was staged. Like mad bulls after a red flag or blood thirsty wolves after a carcass, so did these human wolves called men rave to destroy their fellow citizens. But these brave boys of ours fought gamely and held back the enemy for hours. Owing to the shortage of ammunition they were forced to retreat from Cincinnati, and immediately the advancing force began to pillage and burn that section.

MARY PARRISH

"My Experience in Tulsa"
Events of the Tulsa Disaster, pp. 8–9

THE MASSACRE

FIGURE 1.8
Oklahoma Historical Society
LaQuita Headley Collection

The body of an elderly Black man lies next to what are likely the Frisco railroad tracks. His age suggests that he was one of the many innocent Black Tulsans who were killed merely for being residents of the community. Photo by Yale L. Taplin.

FIGURE 1.9
Tulsa Historical Society and Museum

In one of a series of postcard views captioned "A Victim of the Tulsa Race Riot, June 1, 1921," a group of male onlookers stand over the corpse of a race massacre victim. This photo was taken one block from the Frisco Railroad depot, where some of the heaviest gunfire between Blacks and whites occurred.

As with lynching images, whites were not ashamed to be photographed alongside Black victims. White men who posed for such photos saw themselves as defenders of white womanhood and exemplars of white masculine courage. Photo by Francis Albert Schmidt.

FIGURE 1.10
Tulsa Historical Society and Museum

In this version of the photo, also created as a postcard and using the same caption, the image has been cropped to put the focus more directly on the victim's corpse. Photo by Francis Albert Schmidt.

FIGURE I.II
Tulsa Historical Society and Museum

The body of a massacre victim lies in an alley near the Frisco depot. A handwritten note on the back of this photo reads "A casualty. Tulsa Race Riot, June 1, 1921." Photo by Francis Albert Schmidt.

FIGURE I.12
Northeastern State University Archives
Halliburton Collection

A side view of the same victim taken by a different photographer. A shoe and other personal effects can be seen scattered near the body. Both professional and amateur white photographers made sure to take photos of Black massacre victims before their bodies were picked up.

FIGURE 1.13
Tulsa Historical Society and Museum

This particularly grisly photo, likely produced as a postcard, shows the charred corpse of a race massacre victim lying near the Frisco depot. Rampaging whites set fire to buildings in which Blacks fleeing the violence and destruction had taken refuge, leaving them with no way to escape. Photo by Francis Albert Schmidt.

After the fighting ended and Black survivors were taken away and interned, the grim task of clearing bodies from the streets began. Some Blacks killed during the massacre were hastily buried in cemeteries, while others were likely dumped in mass graves.

Then came the great unthinkable, unspeakable climax. The White people went into those homes just vacated, carried away everything of value, opened safes, destroyed all legal papers and documents, then set fire to the buildings to hide their crime.

P. S. THOMPSON
physician and president of the
Tulsa Medical, Dental, and
Pharmaceutical Association

June 22, 1921
Parrish, *Events of the Tulsa Disaster*, p. 30

I saw my piano and all of my elegant furniture piled in the street. My safe had been broken open, all of the money stolen, also my silverware, cut glass, all of the family clothing, and everything of value had been removed, even my family Bible. My electric light fixtures were broken, the dishes that were not stolen were broken, the floors were covered (literally speaking) with glass, even the phone was torn from the wall. In the basement we gathered two tubs of broken glass from off the floor. My car was stolen and most of my large rugs were taken. I lost seventeen houses that paid me an average of over $425.00 per month.

DR. R. T. BRIDGEWATER
Assistant County Physician

June 22, 1921
Parrish, *Events of the Tulsa Disaster*, p. 34

FIGURE I.15
Tulsa Historical Society and Museum
Beryl D. Ford Collection

A group of white onlookers (far lower right) watch as two white men prepare to enter and presumably loot the home of Ellis and Mary Woods at 531 North Detroit Avenue. Once looters had taken what they wanted from a house, it would be set ablaze.

FIGURE 1.16
Tulsa Historical Society and Museum

A large group of whites watch idly as another home in the 500 block of North Detroit Avenue is looted in preparation for being torched. At far right are some household items that have been placed on the street.

About 1:30 o'clock the firing had somewhat subsided and it was hoped that the crisis had passed over. Some one on the street cried out, "Look, they are burning Cincinnati!" On looking we beheld columns of smoke and fire and by this we knew that the enemy was surging quickly upon Greenwood.

MARY PARRISH   "My Experience in Tulsa"
                                                Events of the Tulsa Disaster, p. 9

Shortly after daylight on Wednesday, June 1, 1921, I received a call to come to the hospital to dress two wounded men. I dressed hurriedly and started to the hospital. Just as I opened my front door a shot was fired at me from a nearby hill, the bullet grazed my leg. I shut the door. A few moments later my wife, hearing the shots,slightly opened the door and a second volley was fired. At this time the shots struck the porch. We shut the door and my wife said, "Doctor, let us go, our lives are worth more than everything." I sat my cases down in the hall and my wife and niece hurriedly dressed, locked the house and departed.

Shortly after we left a whistle blew. The shots rang from a machine gun located on the Stand Pipe Hill near my residence and aeroplanes began to [f]ly over us, in some instances very low to the ground. A cry was heard from the women saying, "Look out for the aeroplanes, they are shooting upon us." The shots continued to be fired in rapid succession from high powered guns from the vicinity of the hill. We continued to flee until we were about two miles northeast of the city. There we tarried at the home of a friend. Shortly the fire broke out, the bullets continued to whistle. The fire grew rapidly, we saw it spreading over our entire district south of the hill.

DR. R. T. BRIDGEWATER
Assistant County Physician

June 22, 1921
Parrish, *Events of the Tulsa Disaster*, p. 33

FIGURE 1.17
Tulsa Historical Society and Museum
Beryl D. Ford Collection

Black Tulsans stand together in the street, observing the smoke from burning homes and buildings filling the air in the Greenwood District. The caption's reference to "running the Negro out of Tulsa" is a clear indication that to some, at least, the actions of the white mob and local authorities represented a concerted attempt to expel the city's Black community.

THE MASSACRE

FIGURE 1.18
University of Tulsa, McFarlin Library

An armed "protector" and three other
white men roam the smoke-filled
Greenwood District.

FIGURE I.19
Tulsa Historical Society and Museum

A young white male holding two shotguns poses for the camera as the Dreamland Theatre burns behind him.

THE MASSACRE

Two armed white men casually walk away
from the burning Greenwood District,
past curious spectators heading toward the
scene of destruction.

FIGURE 1.21
University of Tulsa, McFarlin Library

Whites who took photos during the race massacre made an effort to get panoramic views to capture the magnitude of the destruction. This aerial view was taken from atop a building looking north from First Street. In the foreground is the Tulsa Machine and Tool Company, located at 415 East First Street. The Goodner-Malone Produce Building, located at 1 North Frankfort Avenue, is also visible. "Little Africa" was one of the many racial epithets white Tulsans used in describing Greenwood. They also referred to the area as "Darktown." Such captions make apparent the racism embedded in race massacre photos as well as white resentment of Greenwood's thriving community.

FIGURE I.22
Tulsa Historical Society and Museum

In this postcard photo, a seemingly relaxed group of white men take in the sight of smoke billowing from the Greenwood District. At center is a member of the Oklahoma National Guard. Instead of putting out fires in Greenwood or rounding up whites who were looting and burning homes and businesses, white guardsmen joined in the destruction.

The thing that I remember more than anything is in our house, which was right next door to Mount Zion Baptist Church. My mother was with her family, four children—two boys and two girls. All of us were in the house—and I've told this story over and over again—when we saw, coming up the walk at the front of the house off of Easton Street, four men with torches in their hands. Those torches were burning. When my mother saw them coming, she said Get up under the bed! Get up under the bed! Get up under the bed! And all four of us got up under the bed.

They set our house on fire. They went straight to the curtains and set the curtains on fire. And as a result that's how our house first started to burning.

GEORGE MONROE

interviewed April 16, 1999
Tulsa Race Riot Survivors' Stories, tape 1, pp. 3–4

BURNING OF CHURCH WHERE AMUNC...
WAS STORED - DURING TULSA RAC...

FIGURE I.23
Tulsa Historical Society and Museum

The rumor that the newly built Mount Zion Baptist Church was used as a munitions storehouse has never been confirmed, but Black riflemen did take aim at invading whites from the church's tower, which provided a clear view of the area below. Whites subsequently machine-gunned the tower and then set the church on fire. At the time of the massacre, the congregation had been holding services in the new church for less than two months. They still owed $50,000 of the $92,000 construction cost.

FIGURE 1.24
University of Tulsa, McFarlin Library

Mount Zion Baptist Church on fire,
with smoke pouring from the windows
and the roof.

FIGURE 1.25
Tulsa Historical Society and Museum

As Mount Zion Baptist Church went up
in flames, parishioners hastily placed
church property on the street to protect
it from being destroyed.

FIGURE 1.26
University of Tulsa, McFarlin Library

White Tulsans look on as Mount Zion
Baptist Church is consumed by flames.

FIGURE 1.27
University of Tulsa, McFarlin Library

Only the outer brick walls of Mount Zion
Baptist Church survived the fire.

FIGURE 1.28
Tulsa Historical Society and Museum

The ruins of Mount Zion Baptist Church.
Photo by Reverend Jacob H. Hooker, who
was also a professional photographer.

If we had had complete cooperation from the officers of Tulsa they could have prevented all this disaster, and not use the occasion to demoralize our business industries and our nice homes, but instead of protection it was seemingly a matter of destroy and abolish all Negro business and nice residences.

A. J. NEWMAN

June 24, 1921
Parrish, *Events of the Tulsa Disaster*, pp. 38, 41

Little is recognizable along Greenwood
Avenue after the inferno.

FIGURE 1.30
Greenwood Cultural Center

The burned-out shell of the Dreamland
Theatre.

Pointing his camera up Greenwood
Avenue from Archer Street, the creator
of this photograph captured a stark
view of the devastation.

FIGURE 1.32
Tulsa Historical Society and Museum

The extent of the destruction is evident in this group of photos taken by *Tulsa World* staff photographer Clarence Jack (figures 1.32–1.34). Among the businesses that were lost were the Dixie Theatre and the offices of the Black-owned Tulsa Star newspaper at 120 North Greenwood. The stamps at top right indicate that these images were used as evidence in a grand jury investigation into the causes of the race massacre and in the subsequent court case involving Tulsa police chief John Gustafson. Gustafson was found guilty of dereliction of duty in connection with the massacre and removed from office.

FIGURE I.33
Tulsa Historical Society and Museum

FIGURE I.34
Tulsa Historical Society and Museum

FIGURE 1.35
University of Oklahoma Libraries
C. B. Clark Photograph Collection

A white couple have their picture taken
in front of one of the burned-out
buildings in the Greenwood District,
memorializing their connection to the
thwarted "negro uprising."

FIGURE 1.36
University of Oklahoma Libraries
C. B. Clark Photograph Collection

Against a backdrop of desolation, a
white man seemingly poses behind some
downed electrical wires on Greenwood
Avenue. The whites who came to gawk at
the destruction did little to help the
community rebuild after the massacre.

FIGURE 1.37
Oklahoma Historical Society
Ella Mahler Collection

The remnants of iron bed frames lie atop
the debris from a burned-out building.

THE MASSACRE

We lost everything. Everything that we owned was burned to the ground! What I miss most were the family photos that we had in our house. My father had lots of photographs of family in our house, and those can never be replaced.

BINKLEY WRIGHT

interviewed August 25, 2000
"Meet the Survivors," Tulsa Reparations Coalition
https://tulsareparations.z19.web.core.windows.
net/BWright.htm

Charred trees stand out in a section of the Greenwood District that has otherwise been completely leveled. Visible in the back right corner of the photo is one of the American Red Cross tents that were issued to massacre survivors.

FIGURE 1.39
Tulsa Historical Society and Museum

Looking eastward, this wide-angle
view reveals several blocks of destroyed
homes and businesses within the
Greenwood District.

Within the photograph (handwritten): TULSA NEGRO UPRISING
LOOKING SOUTH FROM BRISK PLANT

FIGURE 1.40
Oklahoma Historical Society

From an elevated position at the brick plant off Elgin Avenue, photographer Clarence Jack panned to the south to capture the devastation.

Even women with shopping bags would come in, open drawers, take every kind of finery from clothing to silverware and jewelry. Men were carrying out the furniture, cursing as they did so, saying "These d— Negroes have better things than lots of white people." . . . Then the horde of ruffians went down on Detroit, looting those beautiful homes of everything valuable and then burned them, even breaking the phones from the walls. The machine guns just shattered the walls of the homes. The fire department came out and protected the White homes on the west side of Detroit Street while on the east side of the street men with torches and women with shopping bags continued their looting and burning of Negro homes.

ANONYMOUS SURVIVOR
("Name withheld by request")

June 24, 1921
Parrish, *Events of the Tulsa Disaster*, pp. 41–42

Ruins of best homes in Tulsa colored section.

FIGURE 1.41
Oklahoma Historical Society

The Black residences on North Detroit Avenue—the "best homes" in the city's "colored section"—once stood as a symbol of progress and achievement. More than a thousand homes in the Greenwood District were burned to the ground during the rampage. Photo by Clarence Jack.

2

Internment

Someone called up our home and said for the men not to fight, for the Home Guard were visiting the homes and searching them, but that they would harm no one. A few minutes after that some men appeared with drawn guns and ordered all men out of the house. I went out immediately. They ordered me to raise my hands, after which three or four men searched me. They told me to line up in the street. I requested them to let me get my hat and best shoes but they refused and abusively ordered me to lineup. They refused to let one of the men put on any kind of shoes. After lining up some 30 or 40 of us men they ran us through the streets to Convention Hall, forcing us to keep our hands in the air all the while. While we were running some of the ruffians would shoot at our heels and swore at those who had difficulty in keeping up. They actually drove a car into the bunch and knocked down two or three men.

When we reached Convention Hall we were searched again. There people were herded in like cattle. The sick and wounded were dumped out in front of the building and remained without attention for hours.

JAMES T. A. WEST

June 20, 1921
Parrish, *Events of the Tulsa Disaster*, p. 24

When the riot came I was at the school getting ready for the prom. When I found out what was happening I went looking for my dad. He was on top of our building shooting back. A lot of Black men were up there, even the white guy who ran the movie projector at the Dreamland for my dad. He told the white man to get me out of there, he would be along shortly. I ran down the Midland [Valley Railroad] tracks, but we got separated. Later some white men stopped me. They said "you got a gun boy." I said no. "Take that off," they said. Two of them marched me to Convention Hall and the other continued patrolling down the Midland Valley railroad tracks. I was there three or four days. I didn't know if my parents were living or dead.

W. D. WILLIAMS

No interview date provided
"Meet the Survivors," Tulsa Reparations Coalition, https://tulsareparations.z19.web.core.windows.net /Eyewitness.htm

FIGURE 2.1
Tulsa Historical Society and Museum

An armed white man strides authoritatively between Black detainees being moved to a detention center. During the race massacre, as many as five hundred white men were appointed as special deputies with the power to arrest and even kill Black people.

FIGURE 2.2
Tulsa Historical Society and Museum
Beryl D. Ford Collection

A group of Black citizens are detained by several armed white men, perhaps while trying to leave Tulsa after the Oklahoma National Guard declared martial law in the city on June 1. The two cars blocking the road appear to have been used to create a makeshift checkpoint. The Red Cross estimated that more than seven hundred Black families temporarily left Tulsa during and immediately following the race massacre. Some never returned.

FIGURE 2.3
Tulsa Historical Society and Museum

A white police officer (left) and a private white citizen walk a detained Black man past a small group of Black onlookers.

The avowed purpose of this invasion was to disarm the Negroes and to corral the men or arrest them that they might not do any further harm. They (the Whites) did this and in most cases met with no resistance except in cases where no reason was given by the Whites for entering the Negro homes, and this was generally the rule. The Negro did not know whether he was being called out to be shot, or what, for shooting was all he could hear or see. If he submitted without question he was taken to jail, but if he dared to question the intruder he was shot.

P. S. THOMPSON
physician and president of the
Tulsa Medical, Dental, and
Pharmaceutical Association

June 22, 1921
Parrish, *Events of the Tulsa Disaster*, pp. 29–30

FIGURE 2.4
University of Tulsa, McFarlin Library

In this and the photo opposite, detained
Blacks are searched for weapons in the
residential section of the Greenwood
District. Photo by Joseph McMinn Hause.

FIGURE 2.5
University of Tulsa, McFarlin Library

Photo by Joseph McMinn Hause.

97

FIGURE 2.6
University of Tulsa, McFarlin Library

Figures 2.6–2.9 show that entire families were loaded onto trucks and transported under armed guard to detention centers. Photo by Joseph McMinn Hause.

Photo by Joseph McMinn Hause.

FIGURE 2.8
University of Tulsa, McFarlin Library

Photo by Joseph McMinn Hause.

FIGURE 2.9
University of Tulsa, McFarlin Library

Photo by Joseph McMinn Hause.

FIGURE 2.10
University of Tulsa, McFarlin Library

The detainees were taken to Convention
Hall in downtown Tulsa until it
was filled to capacity. Photo by Joseph
McMinn Hause.

Our men were all disarmed as soon as caught. About 11 o'clock the enemy took my invalid mother and one of my sisters, supposedly to send them to Convention Hall for safety. Another sister and I scouted about until one o'clock when along came a truck and picked me up and carried me to Convention Hall where I stayed until about 2 o'clock. On entering Convention Hall I failed to find my mother so I went in search for her. With the aid of the Red Cross I found her that night at the North Methodist Church.

MRS. CARRIE KINLAW

June 20, 1921
Parrish, *Events of the Tulsa Disaster*, p. 24

A shirtless Black man is guarded by
military personnel and armed white
citizens. The truck is stopped in front of
the Litan Hotel, located at 21 A West
Second Street. Photo by Arthur Dudley.

FIGURE 2.12
University of Tulsa, McFarlin Library

With white men standing guard on the
side rails, a lumber truck that has been
repurposed to transport Black detainees
travels past 6 North Main Street on its way
through downtown Tulsa, likely on the
way to Convention Hall. Photo by Francis
Albert Schmidt.

FIGURE 2.13
University of Tulsa, McFarlin Library

White authorities used any means available to transport the more than four thousand Blacks who were taken to detention sites. This group was being transported in the bed of a wagon.

Even children had to raise their hands in the air to show that they had no weapons and posed no threat. Photo by Francis Albert Schmidt.

I was lost from my daughter and her baby until late in the afternoon Wednesday. I saw about five women faint. At the Presbyterian Church I saw about four little children who were lost from their mothers. Old and young had to pile on trucks and when we were being driven through town men were seen clapping their hands rejoicing over our condition.

MRS. ROSEATTER MOORE

June 20, 1921
Parrish, *Events of the Tulsa Disaster*, p. 29

FIGURE 2.14
Tulsa Historical Society and Museum

With an obviously distraught Black
woman perched on the back and a white
man literally riding shotgun on the
passenger-side running board, a truck
carries a group of Black Tulsans toward
an uncertain future. In addition to the
trauma of being taken from their homes
and moved to internment sites, many
detainees became separated from their
families in the massacre's aftermath.
Some of the missing were reunited with
their loved ones at the detention centers;
others, however, were never located. This
uncaptioned postcard photo by Alvin
Krupnick was published in the *New York
Times* as a powerful evocation of the
distress and desperation experienced by
survivors of the race massacre.

FIGURE 2.15
Tulsa Historical Society and Museum

As this and the photo on the following page show, white civilians took obvious pleasure in the authority granted to them by the police, forcing the "captives" they rounded up to march with their hands raised in submission.

FIGURE 2.16
University of Tulsa, McFarlin Library

A bunch of Whites came down from the hill. My wife and I ventured out amidst the volley of fire, met them about a block from home and told them that my wife was sick and I did not want to leave her. They had me to raise my hands and searched me. I was bare-headed—one did not want me to even get my hat, but my wife threw it to me. The Lieutenant who was leading them assured me that my wife and baby would be safe and that my home would not be molested. Then I was marched to the top of the brick yard hill and there I was called all kinds of names by boys from 10 years to men of 60. Then I was loaded on a truck and carried to the corner of Boulder and Brady Streets and here I was taken off the truck and searched again; cursed, called all kinds of names in the language of "Take your hats off," "Throw up your hands," "Be submissive and obey to the letter." Even boys of 10. I obeyed.

A. J. NEWMAN

June 20, 1921
Parrish, *Events of the Tulsa Disaster*, pp. 37–38

FIGURE 2.17
Tulsa Historical Society and Museum

As this and the photo opposite show, white onlookers seemed to enjoy the public spectacle of Black Tulsans being herded through the streets.

FIGURE 2.18
Oklahoma State University–Tulsa Library
Ruth Sigler Avery Collection

INTERNMENT

Within the image: THE CONTINENTAL

*NATIONAL GUARDS - TAKING NEGROS TO BALL
PARK FOR PROTECTION - RACE RIOT AT TUL
JUNE 1ST 1921*

FIGURE 2.19
Western History Collections,
University of Oklahoma Libraries

Once Convention Hall was full, detained Black Tulsans were taken to the fairgrounds or McNulty Park. Here a group of detainees pass the Continental Supply Company at 19 South Main Street on their way to the park, being escorted by Oklahoma National Guardsmen "for protection." The postcard's ironic caption stands in stark contrast to the lived experiences of Black Tulsans, whose lives, homes, and businesses were destroyed while white authorities did nothing to stem the violence. The "protection" offered Blacks following the massacre entailed their being removed from their homes at gunpoint and forcibly marched to detention centers.

Typical scene at McNulty park.

FIGURE 2.20
University of Tulsa, McFarlin Library

In this "typical scene," Black survivors of the race massacre have been brought to McNulty Park, where they will be searched again and detained.

FIGURE 2.21
University of Tulsa, McFarlin Library

Normally home to a minor-league baseball team, McNulty Park, located on Elgin Avenue between 9th and 10th Streets, was used after the massacre to intern survivors.

Pictured here is the entrance to McNulty Park. Black race massacre survivors wait patiently in a single file line as white Tulsans who may have burned and looted Greenwood homes and businesses are now overseeing their internment. As Black survivors are once again searched for weapons and valuables, they are given milk and bread. For many survivors, this was likely the first meal they'd had since the massacre had erupted.

FIGURE 2.23
University of Tulsa, McFarlin Library

A group of Black men being moved to
a detention center are escorted by the
National Guard through a pristine white
neighborhood. The image of an untouched white residential area stands in
stark contrast to the complete destruction
of the Greenwood District.

They [Oklahoma National Guardsmen] marched us from there down Pine to Cincinnati, from Cincinnati and Pine down to where—downtown on Brady—the Convention Hall and when we got there they searched us before they would let us go in. And my mother had picked up my oldest brother's service revolver before we left. I had a little satchel she put it in and they wanted to see it. And she said, "I don't have anything in here but some important papers." And one of them said, "The young ones got new tricks like the old ones." So they searched the bag and took the pistol and gave her the bag back.

EUNICE JACKSON

interviewed May 7, 1999
Tulsa Race Riot Survivors' Stories, tape 3, p. 34

FIGURE 2.24
Tulsa Historical Society and Museum

Oklahoma National Guardsmen march past 124 South Main Street in downtown Tulsa. The Security Building, previously known as the First National Bank Building, is in the background.

The detainees they were escorting were likely headed for Convention Hall. A handwritten note on the back of the photo reads "State militia on riot duty at 2nd and Main St., Tulsa, June 1, 1921."

FIGURE 2.25
Tulsa Historical Society and Museum

White spectators look on from a nearby street corner as several detained families are moved to Convention Hall. White onlookers yelled at, mocked, and taunted Black detainees as they were marched through the streets.

FIGURE 2.26
Tulsa Historical Society and Museum
Beryl D. Ford Collection

The photo used for this postcard depicting "captured Negros" being marched by white civilians to Convention Hall was likely taken downtown on South Main Street. Although the detainees had surrendered to armed whites, the caption illustrates the great pride that white men took in putting Black men on public display whom they believed they had emasculated. Photo by Charles L. Reeder.

FIGURE 2.27
Tulsa Historical Society and Museum

Completed in 1914, Convention Hall
(now the Tulsa Theater) was used as
an internment site for Black massacre
survivors.

INTERNMENT

Going to the convention hall that was hard on my family trying to wait to see if my father, whether he was living or not. That was about one of the worst one[s] besides of being in the house that was set on fire, not knowing whether my father was dead or not. That was the worst one.

KINNEY BOOKER

interviewed April 16, 1999
Tulsa Race Riot Survivors' Stories, tape 1, p. 29

FIGURE 2.28
Northeastern State University Archives
Halliburton Collection

This and the photo on the following page show white Tulsans flocking to Convention Hall to take in the spectacle of the Black detainees' arrival and sharing in the triumphant defeat of the "negro uprising."

FIGURE 2.29
Northeastern State University Archives
Halliburton Collection

FIGURE 2.30
Tulsa Historical Society and Museum

Under the close supervision of an armed white man, a Black detainee sits in the bed of a truck next to a deceased massacre victim. The body may have been that of Dr. A. C. Jackson. According to eyewitnesses, the renowned physician and surgeon was killed by special deputies even though he had willingly surrendered. His body was then unceremoniously dumped on the steps of Convention Hall. Photo by Charles L. Reeder.

FIGURE 2.31
Tulsa Historical Society and Museum
Beryl D. Ford Collection

As detainees are moved into Convention
Hall, some of the white onlookers have
climbed up on windowsills, positioning
themselves to get a better view of the
action and capture an unobstructed photo.

About 10 o'clock men came out in cars and told us the troops had come. Shortly afterwards we saw men dressed as soldiers in automobiles rounding up the people and asking them to go back, that they were safe, and on our return my wife and niece were told to go up Greenwood Street and I was searched and told to go in another direction to Convention Hall, where I was marched with hands up and hat off. I was searched with hands up by two or three different sets of officers. I reached Convention Hall about 10:30. On the way to Convention Hall, possibly thirty minutes after the troops came, there was only one small fire north of the hill, but the next day when I viewed the devastated area, there were hundreds of houses burned after the troops had rounded up the men and taken them to Convention Hall.

DR. R. T. BRIDGEWATER

June 22, 1921
Parrish, *Events of the Tulsa Disaster*, p. 33

FIGURE 2.32
Tulsa Historical Society and Museum

A detained Black man is patted down before being taken into Convention Hall. There was no need to frisk newly arrived detainees, as they had already been searched before setting off for the detention site. This second pat-down was thus a calculated performance of power and authority for white onlookers. Photo by Charles L. Reeder.

Then came the unpleasant duty of getting out. You must have some White person to vouch for you, and, of course, I did not know any one (being an architect, my brother and I have contracted and worked for ourselves). So I was up against a hard proposition, but finally I got out through a young fellow who told a man that "This boy is my brother-in-law."

J. C. LATIMER   Parrish, *Events of the Tulsa Disaster*, pp. 44, 47

We went in [and] found a seat and waited. We sat there until about four o'clock when a white family my mother worked for had been there twice and asked about us and she had given our name and we didn't even answer. So then they finally turned us loose.

EUNICE JACKSON

interviewed May 7, 1999
Tulsa Race Riot Survivors' Stories, tape 3, p. 34

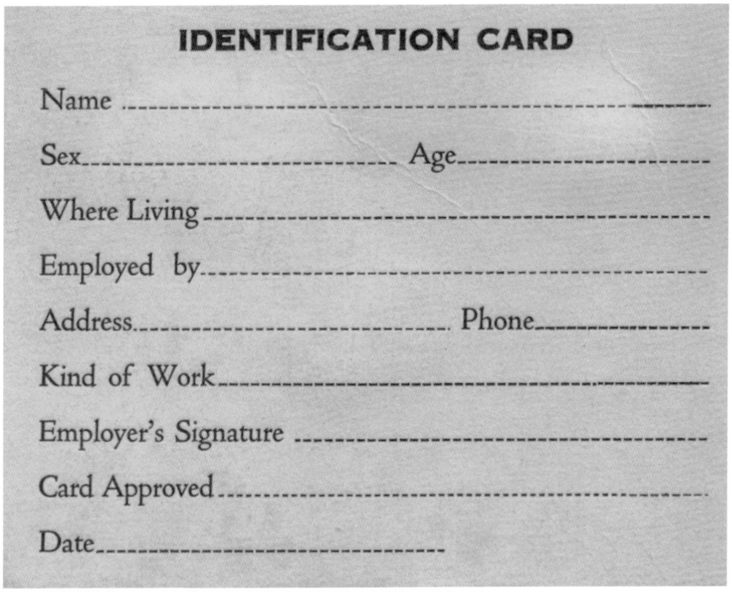

IDENTIFICATION CARD

Name ....

Sex... Age...

Where Living...

Employed by..

Address....................................... Phone...................................

Kind of Work...

Employer's Signature ....

Card Approved ....

Date..

FIGURE 2.33
Tulsa Historical Society and Museum

The American Red Cross issued identification cards to Blacks being held at detention centers. The card pictured here required proof of employment in the form of a signature from an employer. Detainees who had a white employer to vouch for them were released immediately; those who were not in the employ of a white person had to find another white person who could validate their identity and promise that they would be kept inside or at their place of work. After being released, Black Tulsans were forced to carry ID cards for approximately a month following the massacre.

The men had been taken to different places, some to churches and some to the Convention Center. The next day our husbands were brought to the fairgrounds and we were reunited. We sure were glad to see each other. If any white employer called for his Black worker, the worker and his family would be allowed to go home. That's how we got to go home. We heard Thomas' boss calling, "T. R. Davis, T. R. Davis, come on out." Thomas answered and we got to leave.

ROSA DAVIS SKINNER   interviewed in 1994
North Tulsa Oral History Project, transcript, p. 128

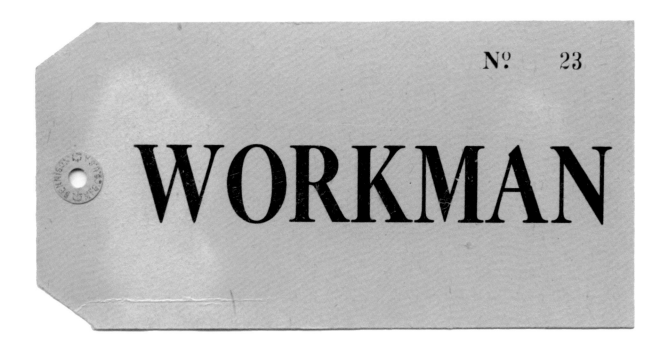

FIGURE 2.34
Tulsa Historical Society and Museum

A workman tag was issued by the Red Cross to Black detainees who had been vouched for by a white employer.

One had to have some white person vouch for them regardless of their station in life before the trouble.... As I had never worked for any white person in Tulsa I was at a loss just what to do. It was plainly shown that a white man's word was the only requirement to receive a card. I pondered just what to do, then I thought of a business firm and called them up. They came down and identified me and that was sufficient. I received my card without any trouble.

MARY PARRISH   "My Experience in Tulsa"
                                         Events of the Tulsa Disaster, pp. 18–19

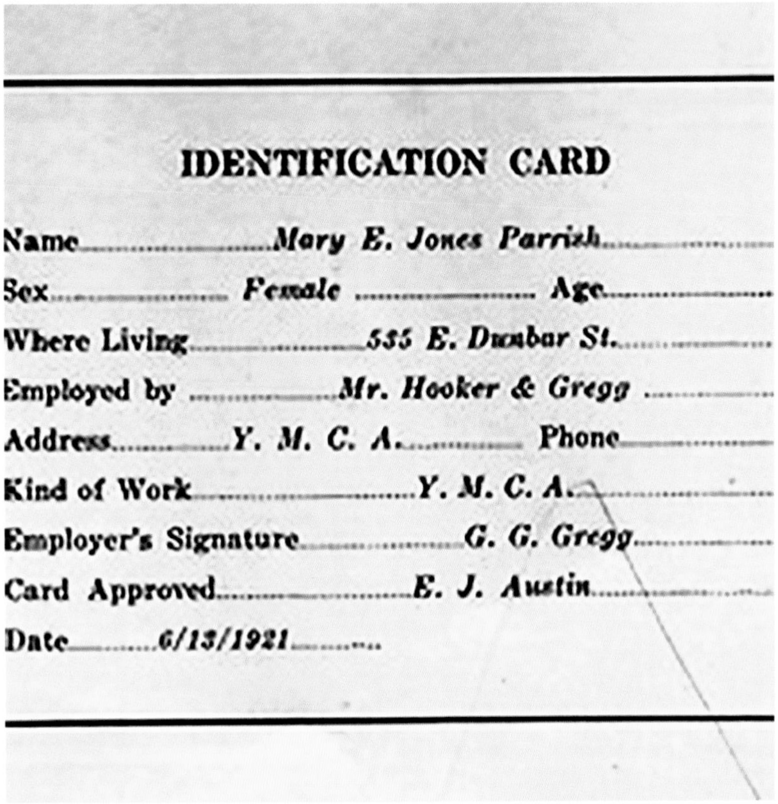

IDENTIFICATION CARD

Name .... *Mary E. Jones Parrish* ....
Sex .... *Female* .... Age ....
Where Living .... *555 E. Dunbar St.* ....
Employed by .... *Mr. Hooker & Gregg* ....
Address .... *Y. M. C. A.* .... Phone ....
Kind of Work .... *Y. M. C. A.* ....
Employer's Signature .... *G. G. Gregg* ....
Card Approved .... *E. J. Austin* ....
Date .... *6/13/1921* ....

FIGURE 2.35
Tulsa Race Riot Photographs

A facsimile of Mary E. Jones Parrish's
identification card. Parrish authored
Events of the Tulsa Disaster (1923), one of
the earliest accounts of the race massacre.

I don't know how they got these cards printed so fast but everyone had little I.D. [identification] cards, even the school children that said who you were and where you was supposed to be. So then you had to have that I.D. where ever you went. And I kept it for awhile but I got rid of it eventually.

EUNICE JACKSON

interviewed May 7, 1999
Tulsa Race Riot Survivors' Stories, tape 3, p. 34

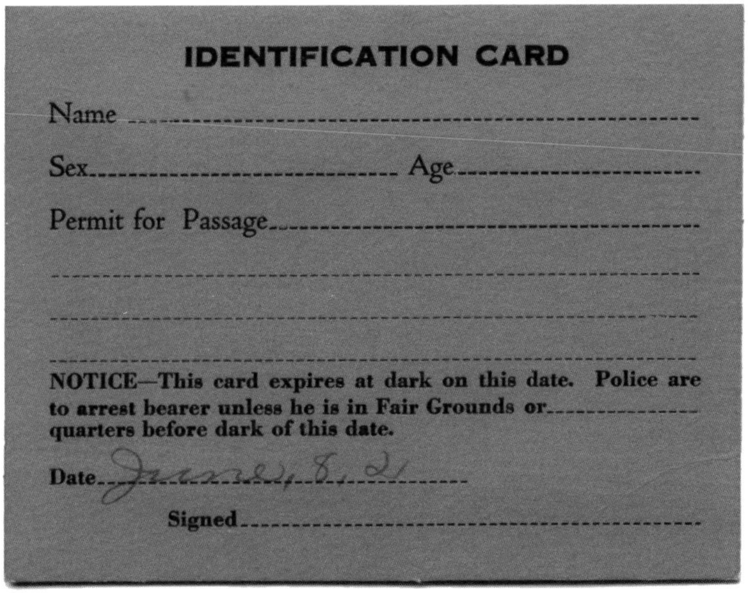

IDENTIFICATION CARD

Name --

Sex----------------------------- Age---------------------

Permit for Passage--------------------------------------

NOTICE—This card expires at dark on this date. Police are
to arrest bearer unless he is in Fair Grounds or-----------
quarters before dark of this date.

Date----*June 8, 21*----------------

Signed---

FIGURE 2.36
Tulsa Historical Society and Museum

Another version of a Red Cross
identification card, this "travel pass" would
have been issued to a detainee who did
not have a white employer. Detained
Blacks were required to carry it at all times
or be subject to arrest. As the text on the
ID implies, the cards were time limited and
had to be reissued once they expired.

The travel pass harkened back to the
days of slavery, when enslaved Blacks
were required to carry a pass signed
by a slaveholder whenever they moved
between plantations or ran errands.
Requiring massacre survivors to carry
a travel pass was an unconstitutional
breach of their civil liberties as well as
a deeply humiliating experience.

FIGURE 2.37
Tulsa Historical Society and Museum

Black detainees were required to present
a Red Cross–issued police protection tag
in order to gain entry to the Greenwood
District in the days following the massacre.

3

Angels of Mercy

After spending such a dreadful night and day and witnessing so much destruction, how could we trust a race that would bring it about? At that hour we mistrusted every person having a white face and blue eyes. Since, we have learned that the Red Cross workers came like angels of mercy to heal and help suffering humanity.

MARY PARRISH

"My Experience in Tulsa"
Events of the Tulsa Disaster, p. 13

Many of us were left helpless and almost hopeless. We sat among the wrack and ruin of our former homes and peered listlessly into space. It was at this time and under such conditions that the American Red Cross—that Angel of love and mercy—came to our assistance.

EDDIE FAYE GATES   *They Came Searching*, p. 274

FIGURE 3.1
Tulsa Historical Society and Museum

Booker T. Washington High School served as Disaster Relief Headquarters for the American Red Cross following the race massacre. From this location, Red Cross staff and relief workers provided medical care, food, tents, and other supplies to assist dislocated Blacks. Maurice Willows, who directed the relief effort, is pictured at far right. Photo by Gifford I. Talmage.

Returning to the Red Cross headquarters I found long rows of women, men and children waiting their turn to receive clothing such as was obtainable. And the thing that I could not understand was why these innocent people, who were as helpless as babes, were placed under guard. Nevertheless, heavily armed guards were all around the building. Some were kind and manly, others were beasts dressed in uniforms. These poor people stood for hours waiting their turn: some were seen to sicken and faint. The nurses would immediately take them out of line and give them treatment.

MARY PARRISH

"My Experience in Tulsa"
Events of the Tulsa Disaster, p. 17

ANGELS OF MERCY

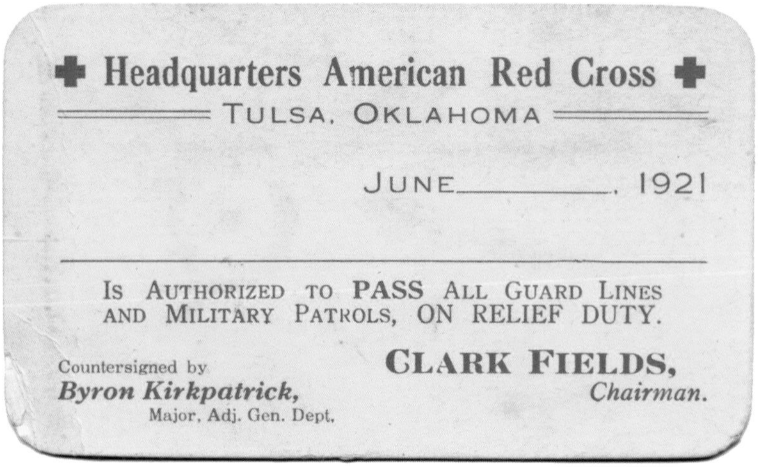

Headquarters American Red Cross
═══ TULSA, OKLAHOMA ═══

JUNE_____, 1921

IS AUTHORIZED TO **PASS** ALL GUARD LINES
AND MILITARY PATROLS, ON RELIEF DUTY.

Countersigned by
Byron Kirkpatrick,   **CLARK FIELDS,**
Major, Adj. Gen. Dept.   *Chairman.*

FIGURE 3.2
Tulsa Historical Society and Museum

This pass was issued to Red Cross workers taking part in the relief effort. It allowed them to move around freely, and they could also use it to obtain one dollar's worth of groceries from any store.

The primary rooms of the Booker Washington School were converted into an emergency hospital. I can never erase the sights of my first visit to the hospital. There were men wounded in every conceivable way, like soldiers after a big battle. Some with amputated limbs, burned faces, others minus an eye or with heads bandaged. There were women who were nervous wrecks, and some confinement cases. Was I in a hospital in France [during World War I]? No, in Tulsa.

MARY PARRISH

"My Experience in Tulsa"
Events of the Tulsa Disaster, p. 19

FIGURE 3.3
Tulsa Historical Society and Museum

Red Cross workers pose in front of one of the four hospital wards at Booker T. Washington High School. The Red Cross provided medical treatment for nearly eight hundred survivors, performing more than 150 surgeries in the first week following the massacre. The school's makeshift wards were necessary because Frissell Memorial Hospital, the only hospital in Tulsa that had served Black residents, was destroyed during the white rampage. Photo by Gifford I. Talmage.

FIGURE 3.4
Tulsa Historical Society and Museum

Red Cross relief worker Clarence Dawson holds a Black infant.

Tulsa Red Cross director Maurice Willows (right), leaning against the railing of a screened-in porch at Booker T. Washington High School, looks on as a Red Cross nurse holds a Black infant who was born in the mothers' ward. Red Cross records document eight cases of premature childbirth among survivors that resulted in the babies' deaths. Records also show that all the pregnant women under the care of the Red Cross had medical complications due to the massacre. Photo by Gifford I. Talmage.

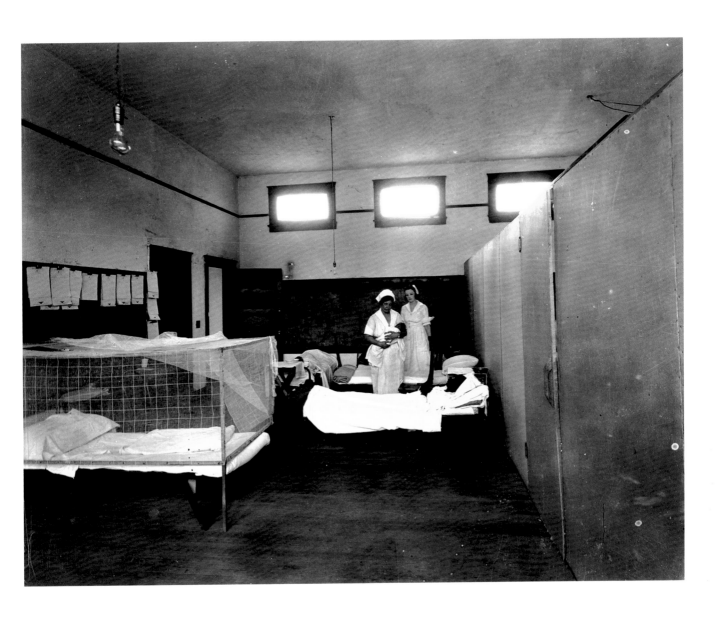

FIGURE 3.6
Tulsa Historical Society and Museum

A nurse holding a Black infant stands
between two patients lying in hospital
beds in a hospital ward at Booker T.
Washington High School. The makeshift
crib at left may indicate that a family
unit was receiving medical care. Photo by
Gifford I. Talmage.

ANGELS OF MERCY

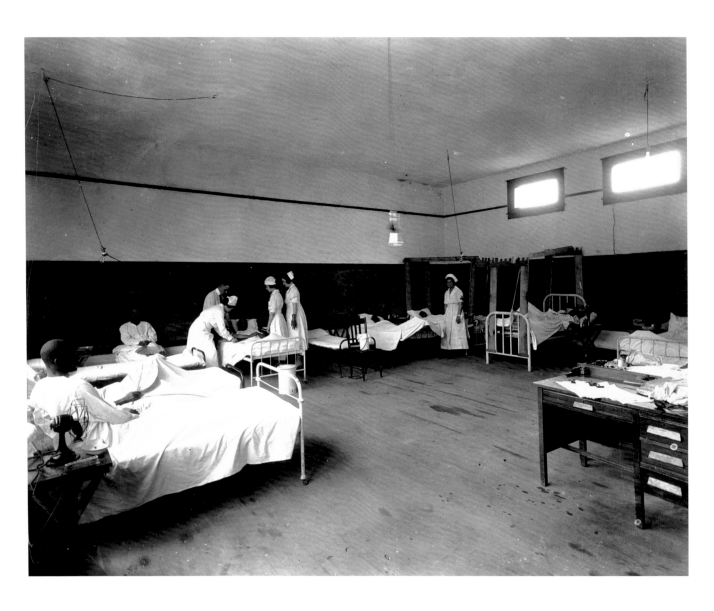

FIGURE 3.7
Tulsa Historical Society and Museum

A team of white doctors and nurses
attend to several Black male patients.
This photograph was likely taken at
Booker T. Washington High School.
Photo by Gifford I. Talmage.

FIGURE 3.8
Tulsa Historical Society and Museum

The Red Cross established a Family Relief Department to assist Black families affected by the massacre. Between June 1 and December 31, 1921, nearly 2,500 families, representing approximately 9,000 survivors, applied for Red Cross relief.

This photograph was likely taken at Booker T. Washington High School. Photo by Gifford I. Talmage.

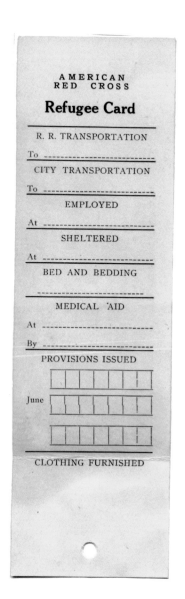

FIGURE 3.9
Tulsa Historical Society and Museum

A refugee card. Issued by the Red Cross to Black survivors, these cards would have been used to document any emergency assistance they received.

FIGURE 3.10
Tulsa Historical Society and Museum

Maurice Willows and a Red Cross staff member photographed during a meeting at Booker T. Washington High School. A notation at the bottom of the photo identifies the location as the "Director's Office." Photo by Gifford I. Talmage.

ANGELS OF MERCY

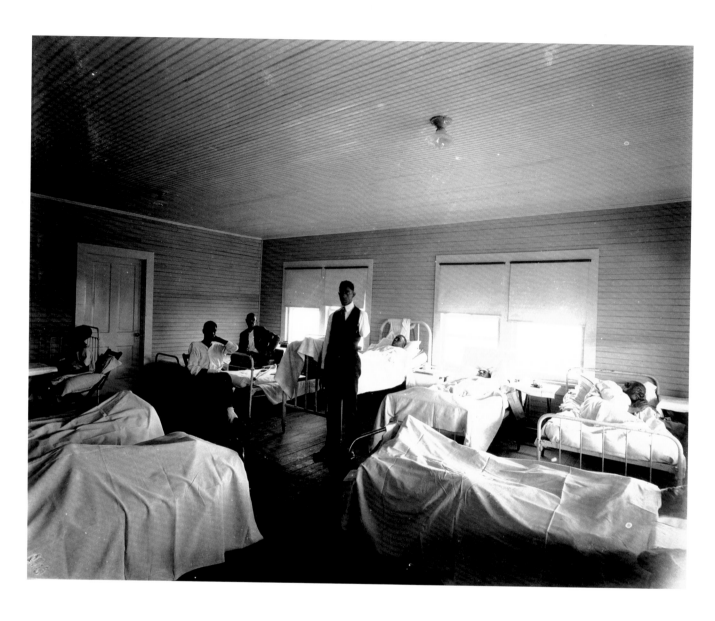

FIGURE 3.11
Tulsa Historical Society and Museum

A ward in the Maurice Willows Hospital, located at 324 North Hartford Street. When the makeshift hospital at Booker T. Washington High School reached capacity, it became apparent that a more permanent solution would be needed. Built with Red Cross funds, the new hospital took the place of the destroyed Frissell Memorial Hospital as the medical facility that served Black Tulsans. In the middle of the photo, a Black man with an amputated arm poses for the camera. Photo by Gifford I. Talmage.

The American Red Cross officially closed its Disaster relief work on December 31, 1921, leaving as a legacy to the colored people the Maurice Willows Hospital, at 324 North Hartford Street. This hospital, as it now stands, is the culmination of the medical relief work done during more troublous times. A great deal of care has been exercised in bringing this institution up to date and making it thoroughly modern, and this hospital probably stands as the most constructive piece of work done by the Red Cross here in Tulsa. Appreciation of it will best be shown by its future, since it is being turned over to the colored race for their operation and management.

MARY PARRISH

"My Experience in Tulsa"
Events of the Tulsa Disaster, p. 76

ANGELS OF MERCY

A request from a true friend.

As you must leave your do entend;

And your leaving is a [re]gret,

As you have done for us—we can never forget.

Please take this as a token

To all whom may concern,

That you came and went as a gentleman,

And the colored of Tulsa will confirm.

When you far away from Tulsa town,

Do not think of us with a frown,

For God only can tell

How much we appreciate you as well

Thank God for the Red Cross,

For by His hand he put you boss,

And thus He would been to blame

If you and your host had not carried out His aim.

Amen.

Poem by massacre survivor and
entrepreneur A. J. Newman, written in
November 1921 as a tribute to Maurice
Willows for his service to survivors,
quoted in Johnson, *Black Wall Street*, p. 236

Records on file in the Red Cross office show that during the seven months between June 1st, and January 1st, they had handled the cases of 2,480 families (8,624 persons), that nearly one-half million feet of lumber and 50,000 yards of cloth were distributed, and that a total expenditure of $100,000 was made for actual relief among the sufferers.

MARY PARRISH

"American Red Cross"
Events of the Tulsa Disaster, p. 76

FIGURE 3.12
Tulsa Historical Society and Museum

Red Cross workers pose for the camera in a Supply Department storeroom at Booker T. Washington High School. In addition to distributing food to massacre survivors, the Red Cross provided household items such as dishes and eating utensils, cots and mattresses, stoves, heaters, lamps, chairs, laundry tubs, and washboards. Photo by Gifford I. Talmage.

FIGURE 3.13
Tulsa Historical Society and Museum

Sewing machines are lined up along one side of a Supply Department storeroom at Booker T. Washington High School. As a cost-saving measure, sewing machines and raw materials were furnished to Black women and girls to enable them to create clothing, quilts, comforters, cot pads, sheets, pillows, and pillowcases. Photo by Gifford I. Talmage.

FIGURE 3.14
Tulsa Historical Society and Museum

In the aftermath of the massacre, there were no restaurants, lunch counters, boardinghouses, or grocery markets at which to obtain food. For most survivors, the Red Cross food supply kept them from starvation. Pictured here is a Red Cross meal voucher, used to procure food and water from the Supply Department.

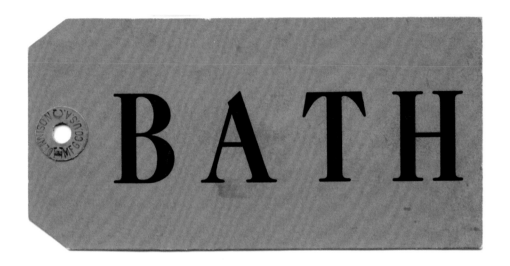

FIGURE 3.15
Tulsa Historical Society and Museum

A bath tag issued by the Red Cross.
It presumably granted destitute Black
survivors access to bathing facilities
as well as soap and other personal
hygiene supplies.

4

Refugees

On the morning of June 1st, I met the mob of Whites at the door where I was. They marched me to Convention Hall with my hands up. From there I was taken to the Ball Park and saw many men and women who were homeless. There I slept on two benches.

I left the park the next morning and looked up my wife who was stopping with some friends. Then I purchased a folding chair, a strop and razor and went down on Greenwood amidst the ashes and ruins and started a barber shop.

From a 10-room and basement modern brick home, I am now living in what was my coal barn. From a 5-chair white enamel barber shop, 4 baths, electric clippers, electric fan, 2 lavatories and shampoo stands, 4 workmen, double marble shine stand, a porter and an income of over $500 or $600 per month, to a razor, strop and folding chair on the sidewalk.

C. L. NETHERLAND   June 24, 1921
                                    Parrish, *Events of the Tulsa Disaster*, p. 42

FIGURE 4.1
Tulsa Historical Society and Museum
Beryl D. Ford Collection

This photo postcard captures the devastation and despair experienced by so many Black families in the space of less than twenty-four hours.

REFUGEES

Upon Standpipe Hill they were shooting from there and where our home was located on Kenosha in the eight hundred block. We were out in the backyard; my father came and had us to come in because the bullets were falling out in the backyard. A fellow, friend of his, a white man, by the name of Sandy McMullin, came over to our home and got the family and took them out to his houses. He live way out on the outskirts of town. I guess that would be I would imagine somewhere in the vicinity where the new Booker T. Washington school is now back in that vicinity. And we stayed there until after this was all over with. When we came back nothing but the ground, home burned down, everything, nothing left.

VENEICE DUNN SIMMS

interviewed April 16, 1999
Tulsa Race Riot Survivors' Stories, tape 1, p. 11

FIGURE 4.2
Oklahoma State University–Tulsa Library
Ruth Sigler Avery Collection

Seated alone in a wooden chair on the bare expanse of ground where her house once stood, an elderly woman appears to be looking around in sadness and disbelief. "An old negro woman sitting in front where her home use to be" is handwritten lightly across the top of the image.

We owned a skating rink there over a large piece of property that we had. And the skating rink during the time of the riot was a large place as to where we were. I remember that is because I learned to skate at five years old. And I had a lot of fun being in the skating rink and helping my father handling the skate keys at five years old and skating and having fun. That was where we kids had [things] then. Now during the riot, it got burned down. Our home got burned down and we had a little rent home next to our house at 410 East Easton Street, which was our home address. And uh, we lost all of this, our property, our home along [with it].

GEORGE MONROE

interviewed April 16, 1999
Tulsa Race Riot Survivors' Stories, tape 1, p. 4

The troops . . . marched all the women and kids up to out on 15th and Harvard were the county fair grounds. And they— put us in there and they gave us a typhoid shot, a tetanus shot, and a shot for measles, and they vaccinated us and kept us out there about four or five days or maybe longer. But in the daytime we could come back over here [to] see if there was anything left that we could salvage. And they had a curfew for the Blacks, after dark we were allowed back over here.

WES YOUNG

interviewed April 16, 1999
Tulsa Race Riot Survivors' Stories, tape 1, p. 47

FIGURE 4.3
Oklahoma Historical Society
Ella Mahler Collection

In a scene that was repeated throughout
the residential section, family members
sift through the rubble of their former
home to collect what is left of their
personal effects and valuables.

As a kid we used to go looking for coins. We'd find money that wasn't too burnt; we'd shine them up and have money. We didn't care whether it was ours or not. Because people had been doing it everywhere.

KINNEY BOOKER

interviewed April 16, 1999
Tulsa Race Riot Survivors' Stories, tape 1, p. 17

REFUGEES

Well my dad, I think one of the reasons they stayed. He had money in a trunk. And for years, we used to chip silver half-dollars and dollars and quarters and things, uh to spend. My kids and I used to . . . have a big ten- or fifteen-pound wad of silver that had been burnt in the race riot and those kids of mine chipped that stuff off and spent it. I got about that much; I'll bring it to you sometimes.

THEODORE PORTERFIELD

interviewed April 16, 1999
Tulsa Race Riot Survivors' Stories, tape 1, p. 36

FIGURE 4.4
National Museum of African American History
and Culture, Gift of Scott Ellsworth

A charred "riot penny" that was recovered
by then five-year-old George Monroe
from among the debris of his family's
home. Charred coins are a tangible
reminder of the worst race massacre in
American history.

REFUGEES

A group consisting primarily of displaced women and children stand outside one of the entrances to the Tulsa Fairgrounds on June 1. The fairgrounds, which at the time were located at Admiral Boulevard and Lewis Avenue, were one of the sites where detained Blacks were taken following the race massacre. More than four thousand survivors were interned at detention camps, and two thousand were held at the fairgrounds.

The soldiers came and had the children and grown ups
to go to the ball park and we were given bread and milk.

CLEO HARDING

interviewed May 17, 1999
Tulsa Race Riot Survivors' Stories, tape 4, p. 30

That riot was a terrible thing. There was so much death and destruction. So much disorder. The National Guard was called to keep the peace. The women in my group had been taken to the fairgrounds and were raising a lot of sand—we were all hungry, thirsty, and just plain scared to death. A milk truck and a bread truck came and brought us some food. We were each given a bottle of sweet milk and some slices of bread. I never did like sweet milk. In fact, I never did drink it. But this day, I was so tired, scared, and thirsty that I drunk that bottle of sweet milk right up!

ROSA DAVIS SKINNER

interviewed in 1994
North Tulsa Oral History Project, transcript, p. 128

FIGURE 4.6
Oklahoma Historical Society
Beryl D. Ford Collection

Reverend Robert A. Whitaker (at left, wearing necktie) helps distribute relief goods to Black refugees displaced by the race massacre. Whitaker was the pastor of Mount Zion Baptist Church.

Well, after the riot, they gave everyone tents. You know, to live in. That's what they were suppose to have to live in. My father took one and he built a floor, you know got wood and made, built a floor and all because he said he wouldn't have us on no ground.

VENEICE DUNN SIMMS

interviewed April 16, 1999
Tulsa Race Riot Survivors' Stories, tape 1, p. 13

Lots of people were living in tents after the race riot. Red Cross helped give tents, I don't remember who helped, whether it was Mr. Wilcox or the Red Cross, who helped us get a tent. We had a tent and we had a floor in our tent. We were lucky enough to get a floor in our tent. Because it had been raining, it looked like it rained and rained, after the race riot as far I remember.

KINNEY BOOKER

interviewed April 16, 1999
Tulsa Race Riot Survivors' Stories, tape 1, p. 17

FIGURE 4.7
Oklahoma Historical Society
Ella Mahler Collection

A canvas tent set up near the site of a
destroyed building.

FIGURE 4.8
Tulsa Historical Society and Museum

A tent erected by the Red Cross to
provide temporary shelter stands next
to the ruins of a building at 105 North
Greenwood Avenue. Owned by Reverend
W. H. Wood, it housed several Black
physicians, real estate offices, and a school
before the massacre.

FIGURE 4.9
Tulsa Historical Society and Museum

A handwritten note on the back of this photograph reads "Ruins of the Titus Bld. N. Greenwood. Owner Mrs. Titus, a widow." The Black woman standing in the rubble surveying the destruction is likely Mrs. Titus. Photo by Reverend Jacob H. Hooker.

FIGURE 4.10
Tulsa Historical Society and Museum

Displaced when their respective law offices were destroyed during the race massacre, attorneys P. A. Chappelle (not pictured), Buck Colbert Franklin (right), and Isaiah H. Spears (left), pictured here with their secretary, Effie Thompson, founded Spears, Franklin & Chappelle and quickly set up this temporary law office at 607 East Archer. This photo was taken on June 6, 1921. By November 1921, the attorneys had relocated their offices to 107½ Greenwood Avenue. The firm represented many of the Greenwood residents who filed massacre-related lawsuits against the city of Tulsa and local insurance companies. Most notably, the firm filed suit in district court to block the enforcement of the city's post-massacre fire ordinance, which would have made it prohibitively expensive for most Greenwood residents to rebuild.

FIGURE 4.11
Tulsa Historical Society and Museum

The East End Relief Committee assisted
the Red Cross in coordinating emergency
relief efforts for Black survivors. In addition, they helped block the fire ordinance
and subsequently aided the reconstruction
of the Greenwood District.

FIGURE 4.12
Tulsa Historical Society and Museum

Within the first week following the massacre, the Red Cross provided approximately three hundred army tents to house displaced Black Tulsans. The tents pictured here were assembled just west of the Red Cross Headquarters at Booker T. Washington High School.

REFUGEES

FIGURE 4.13
Tulsa Historical Society and Museum

The Red Cross also provided flooring, lumber, screen doors, and other materials so that displaced Blacks could build themselves sturdier temporary homes. By December 1921, nearly eight hundred temporary structures had been erected, but at least forty-nine families were still living in army tents. In this photo, a row of temporary structures is bordered by a line of tents. Thousands of Black Tulsans would spend the following winter in their makeshift housing.

FIGURE 4.14
Tulsa Historical Society and Museum

Between June and December 1921, Red Cross workers transformed more than 150 tents into temporary frame homes to provide better living conditions for the refugees. Here the tents have been repurposed to provide roofs for the frame structures.

FIGURE 4.15
Tulsa Historical Society and Museum

According to a note on the back, this photo shows "Indp. [Independence] St. as it was Nov. 3rd." Despite the canvas coverings, these makeshift shelters would not have provided Black refugees with much protection from the approaching winter. Photos by Reverend Jacob H. Hooker.

FIGURE 4.16
Tulsa Historical Society and Museum

Two temporary housing units provided by the Red Cross. The top structure has a house number or address to the right of the door. On the back of the photo a handwritten note reads "Scene on Easton St. People aided by Red Cross." Photos by Reverend Jacob H. Hooker.

FIGURE 4.17
Tulsa Historical Society and Museum

Figures 4.17–4.19 show Black children who were separated from their parents and were under the care of the Red Cross until family members could be identified. According to Red Cross figures, more than four hundred detached persons were widowed or orphaned as a result of the massacre.

FIGURE 4.18
Tulsa Historical Society and Museum

FIGURE 4.19
Tulsa Historical Society and Museum

FIGURE 4.20
Tulsa Historical Society and Museum

A group of children stand in front of a stack of wooden slats that will be used to build temporary homes for survivors of the race massacre.

5

Rebuilding and Renaissance

The colored man of Tulsa built his home not upon sand, but upon an exceedingly great faith, for when fire does break out all he can do is to stand by and see all his earthly possessions go down in ashes. . . . In spite of all the physical and mental handicaps he has wrought well, and though a part of his city lies in ashes, the carpenter's hammer is heard and new lumber in the form of a house flares up in every direction. The Tulsa attitude of the Black man is to build and rebuild.

RICHARD J. HILL   Parrish, *Events of the Tulsa Disaster*, p. 60

They had a hard time getting lumber, whites didn't want to sell them lumber. They had to be sued by a lawyer, [Buck Colbert] Franklin. His son is a very good friend of mine. His father was living here and they had to sue the City to get a release so we could get lumber. They didn't want us to rebuild. That was evident.

KINNEY BOOKER

interviewed April 16, 1999
Tulsa Race Riot Survivors' Stories, tape 3, p. 20

FIGURE 5.1
Northeastern State University Archives
Halliburton Collection

Undeterred by the city's efforts to use a
fire ordinance to block them from rebuilding, the residents of Greenwood rolled up
their sleeves and got to work. After identifying and removing salvageable items,
they undertook the laborious process of
removing debris.

Two Black men pick through a mound of
debris within the shell of the destroyed
Gurley Hotel at 112½ North Greenwood
Avenue, apparently in search of salvageable
bricks. The luxury hotel, built by wealthy
Black entrepreneur O. W. Gurley, was one
of the first business enterprises in the
Greenwood District. It was never rebuilt.

FIGURE 5.3
Tulsa Historical Society and Museum

A group of men stack bricks being salvaged from the ruins of the Phillips Building, located at 117 North Greenwood Avenue, in anticipation of its reconstruction. Prior to the race massacre, the building was home to a cigar store and a billiard hall.

FIGURE 5.4
Tulsa Historical Society and Museum

Materials to be used in reconstructing businesses along North Greenwood Avenue have been assembled on the sidewalk (background) and curb (foreground). The Bryant Building (far left) and Phillips Building (center) have already been rebuilt. Signage for the Commercial Barber Shop, the Shine Parlor (on the left), Neely and Vaden's Billiards (middle), and Percy's Café (far right) is visible.

FIGURE 5.5
Greenwood Cultural Center

Rebuilding Mount Zion Baptist Church.

FIGURE 5.6
Tulsa Historical Society and Museum

A crew of men at work rebuilding the Vernon African Methodist Episcopal Church. These photos of the reconstruction were taken approximately sixty days after the massacre. According to the church's web page, Vernon A.M.E. "is the only standing Black-owned structure from the Historic Black Wall Street era and the only edifice that remains from the worst race massacre in American history. To this day, Vernon A.M.E Church remains a visual reminder of the Massacre and the reconstruction process."

My parents were leading business people on Greenwood. They had rent houses, a garage, a confectionary store, rooming houses and were part owners of a drug store. Ours was the first Black family to own a car. When other Blacks begin to buy them my dad had become a good mechanic from working on his. He opened a garage. . . . We lost everything.

W. D. WILLIAMS

No interview date provided
"Meet the Survivors," Tulsa Reparations Coalition
https://tulsareparations.z19.web.core.windows.net
/Eyewitness.htm

FIGURE 5.7
Greenwood Cultural Center

By the time this photo was taken, the
reconstruction of the Williams Dreamland
Theatre was well under way.

FIGURE 5.8
Library of Congress
American National Red Cross
Photograph Collection

After clearing away the rubble from their destroyed homes, massacre survivors built temporary structures until they could construct a new home. Here tents and temporary homes are visible as far as the eye can see.

FIGURE 5.9
Tulsa Historical Society and Museum

A wide-angle view, most likely looking
eastward from Sunset Hill, showing the
numerous temporary housing units that
replaced homes destroyed during the race
massacre. Photo by Alvin Krupnick.

FIGURE 5.10
Tulsa Historical Society and Museum

Likely taken from Standpipe Hill, this wide-angle view captures some of the temporary structures erected in the Greenwood District to house the refugees. The Frisco Railroad tracks can be seen in the distance. Photo by Alvin Krupnick.

FIGURE 5.11
Tulsa Historical Society and Museum

Six years after Samuel and Lucy Mackey's modest home on Greenwood Avenue was destroyed in the race massacre, they made good on their vow to rebuild, replacing the original structure with the large brick house pictured here. The only remaining home from 1920s Greenwood, it was dismantled and moved to 322 North Greenwood Avenue in 1986, where it was reconstructed, becoming the Mabel B. Little Heritage House. The home is listed on the National Register of Historic Places.

FIGURE 5.12
Tulsa Historical Society and Museum

Greenwood Avenue north from Archer Street, circa 1925. Most of the destroyed businesses have been rebuilt, and the street is once again bustling with cars and pedestrians. In the far back right, the rebuilt Dreamland Theater is visible.

The rebuilding process began quickly, and as of December 30, 1921, according to the Red Cross, the new structures included 764 frame homes, 51 brick or cement buildings, 7 churches, 2 filling stations, and a large theater.

FIGURE 5.13
Tulsa Historical Society and Museum

The Greenwood District, looking north
from Archer, circa 1925. At right is the
three-story Botkin Building, which was
erected on the lot previously occupied
by the Woods Building; at left is the
rebuilt Williams Building, which
belonged to J. W. Williams, the owner
of the Dreamland Theatre.

FIGURE 5.14
Greenwood Cultural Center

Meharry Drugs, located at 101 North
Greenwood. Store owner Reed Rollerson
stands behind the cash register in this
undated photo.

FIGURE 5.15
Greenwood Cultural Center

The Mann Brothers Grocery Store at 920
North Greenwood Avenue. Store owner
J. D. Mann stands at the far right in this
undated photo. Mann Brothers Grocery
was reputed to be the most modern Black-
owned market in the state of Oklahoma.

FIGURE 5.16
Greenwood Cultural Center

Store owner E. L. Goodwin poses
in his Greenwood Haberdashery
at 119 North Greenwood Avenue in
this undated photo. When Goodwin
opened the business following the
massacre, he became the youngest
business owner on Black Wall Street.

FIGURE 5.17
Greenwood Cultural Center

Greenwood circa 1938. By 1942, the district
boasted nearly 250 businesses, exceeding
the number of business that had been in
operation at the time of the race massacre.

FIGURE 5.18
Greenwood Cultural Center

Members of the Saint Monica Drum and
Bugle Corps march along the 100 block of
Greenwood Avenue in this undated photo.

FIGURE 5.19
Greenwood Cultural Center

Mount Zion Baptist Church in 2003. When the original church went up in flames during the race massacre, the congregation resolved not only to rebuild it but also to finish paying off the $50,000 still owed to the creditor who had provided the original construction loan. In November 1942, the final payment was made on that earlier debt. Ten years later, and more than thirty years after the race massacre, the new Mount Zion was dedicated.

6

Remembering
the Survivors

I was so traumatized by
that riot, I don't remember
much about anything,
except for my terror.
I'll never forget that.

RUTH DEAN NASH

I was too young to
personally remember
details of the riot, but
I heard my parents
talk about the riot—
how bad it was,
how it destroyed so
much property that
Blacks had worked so
hard to acquire.

Oh those innocent days of
childhood before the riot.
Nothing was ever the same
after that riot!

DELOIS VADEN RAMSEY

JUANITA SMITH BOOKER

JOHN MELVIN ALEXANDER, 2002
Born December 22, 1919

J. B. BATES, 2002
Born June 13, 1916

All the talk about reparations has helped me clarify my views on that subject. When I am asked whether I favor reparations for riot victims, I say yes I certainly do! If Japanese Americans got reparations for their suffering during World War II, we Black Tulsa Race Riot survivors deserve it for our suffering in 1921. Some of us survivors fought for this country, the USA, in World War II. I was a steward on war ships. I went to Korea near the ending of the war in that country in the east. Yes, I did my duty for this country. I suffered during that Tulsa riot. I feel that I certainly do deserve reparations!

I was only five years old, too young to know the significance of a riot, but I do remember that my mother was so frightened that I knew that something was terribly wrong. The militia took dad and my uncle to detention. While the militia was busy taking the men in the family away, my mother slipped away with my sister Roxanna and me and ran to hide in a chicken house. With us was an old man on a walking stick. While we were running, an airplane flew over real low and someone in the plane shot and killed that old man! My mother often talked about the riot, but my dad NEVER talked about it!

ESSIE LEE JOHNSON BECK, 2002
Born April 29, 1915

JAMES D. BELL, 2002
Born June 12, 1921

My Johnson relatives had acquired 700 acres of land in Arkansas after the Civil War, but there was so much hatred and envy of Black landowners by Southern whites that my family lost all that land. Due to the deliberate racial injustice of taking their land, and threats against Black land owners, my relatives secretly fled Arkansas. One of Mother's brothers had been targeted and would probably have been murdered had the family remained in Arkansas. That is how my mother arrived in Tulsa just in time to become caught up in the worst race riot in American history!

At the time of the Tulsa riot, my father J. D. (Dick Bell) and my mother, Ida Mae Bell lived at 418 North Cincinnati Avenue in Tulsa. My mother was eight months pregnant with me. Dad and mother came from Missouri to Tulsa in 1918 to get in on the oil boom successes there. Dad was a chauffeur for rich whites such as Tate Brady, Judge Shea, and the owner of Crosby Farms. When the riot started, mother and dad fled along the Santa Fe Railroad tracks, with other fleeing Black refugees all the way to Mohawk Indian Nation Park. Dad had always been fascinated with the police force.

Appointments of Blacks to the police force had always been "political plum" appoinments in return for support of the winning political party at the time. In 1925, two Tulsa commissioners, Thomas I. Monroe and A. P. Bowles, Democrats, recommended that my dad be appointed to the police force. In the next election, the Republicans won and Dad lost his job. The next election a Democrat won and Dad was back on the force.

REMEMBERING THE SURVIVORS

JUANITA SMITH BOOKER
Born January 15, 1914

Everything about that riot was terrible. I remember that we were all riding on a flatbed truck trying to escape the approaching mobs. The truck was going so fast. The driver made a sharp turn on a corner and hit the curb. A lady fell off the truck and was killed! With all this talk in recent years about the Tulsa riot, I have been thinking a lot about my childhood days, both before the riot, during the riot, and after the riot. I remember a little playmate named Juanita Scott, survivor now living in Chicago. At the time of the riot, we lived near the Samuel Jackson Funeral Home on Archer Street. The Scott family lived nearby. Oh those innocent days of childhood before the riot. Nothing was ever the same after that riot!

KINNEY I. BOOKER
Born March 21, 1913

JOHNNIE L. GRAYSON BROWN, 2002
Born July 5, 1914

At the time of the Tulsa Race Riot of 1921, my parents and the five of us children lived at 320 North Hartford Avenue. We had a lovely home, filled with beautiful furniture, including a grand piano. All our clothes and personal belongings—just everything—were burned up during the riot. Early on the morning of June 1, 1921, my parents were awakened by the sounds of shooting and the smell of fire, and the noise of fleeing Blacks running past our house. My dad awakened us children and sent us to the attic with our mother. We could hear what was going on below. We heard the white men ordering dad to come with them; he was being taken to detention. We could hear dad pleading with the mobsters. He was begging them "please don't set my house on fire." But, of course, that is exactly what they did just before they left with dad. Though dad went outside the house with the mobsters, he slipped away from them when they got preoccupied splashing gasoline or kerosene on the outside of the house to speed up the burning. He rushed to the attic and rescued us. We slipped into the crowd of fleeing Black refugees. Thank God we did not burn up in that attic!

I was seven years old when the riot broke out. Some of the riot survivors my age remember a lot about the riot. But I just can't remember much about it. I guess it was so horrible, that my mind has just blotted it out. I just can't remember much about that awful riot.

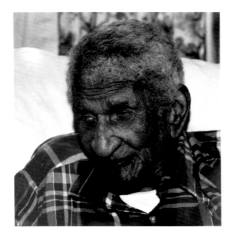

CLARENCE BRUNER, 2002
Born July 28, 1904

JOE BURNS, 2002
Born February 5, 1915

When the riot broke out, I was a teenager working as a bellhop at the Mills Hotel in downtown Tulsa. We made good money. Tulsa was a booming oil town and people were always coming to Tulsa. Hotels, restaurants, entertainment places, taxis, shoe shine parlors, department stores, banks, churches (so many on Boulder Avenue that it was called Cathedral Row)—all profited in the booming oil town. And then came the riot!

On the day of the riot, I remember running with my parents, siblings, and other fleeing Blacks will never forget how cold and scared I was that night. People ask me how I feel about reparations for riot survivors. I am all for it! It is time to rectify the wrongs of the past. It is long past time for healing and justice! That riot was like a first "war experience" for me. We were under attack and our government did not protect us. During WWII, I fought in my first real war. On April 2, 1944, my unit landed in Australia. Two days later, General Douglas MacArthur arrived. Yes, I've done my duty. It is time for those in the United States, the state of Oklahoma, and the city and county of Tulsa to acknowledge culpability for the failure to protect Black people from lynchers and mobsters.

OTIS GRANVILLE CLARK, 2002
Born February 13, 1903

WORDIE "PEACHES" MILLER COOPER, 2002
Born February 4, 1911

I got caught right in the middle of that riot! Some white mobsters were holed up in the upper floor of the Ray Rhee Flour Mill on East Archer and they were just gunning down Black people, just picking them off like they were swatting flies. Well I had a friend who worked for Jackson's funeral home and he was trying to get to that new ambulance so he could drive it to safety. I went with him. He had the keys in his hand, ready for the takeoff. But one of the mobsters in the Rhee building zoomed in on him and shot him in the hand. The keys flew to the ground and blood shot out of his hand and some of it sprayed on me. We both immediately abandoned plans to save that ambulance! We ran for our lives. We never saw my stepfather again, nor our little pet bulldog, Bob. I just know they perished in that riot. My stepfather was a strong family man. I know he did not desert us. I just wish I knew where he was buried.

CARRIE HUMPHREY CUDJOE, 2002
Born April 6, 1913

ERNESTINE GIBBS, 2002
Born December 15, 1902

My parents, David and Hattie Humphrey, moved from Ft. Gibson, Oklahoma to Tulsa. At the time of the riot, they lived at 2111 North Lansing Avenue in a home which they owned. They attended the Holiness Church on the corner of Marshall and Lansing. The pastor was Reverend Nichols. There were six children then. We had a house, a horse, a cow, and some chickens. Our house was burned down during the riot and we lost everything that we had. That riot was an awful thing. It scarred us.

A family friend came from a hotel on Greenwood where he worked and knocked on our door. He was so scared he could not sit still, nor lie down. He just paced up and down the floor talking about the "mess" going on downtown and on Greenwood. When daylight came, Black people were moving down the train tracks like ants. We joined the fleeing people. During this fleeing frenzy we made it to Golden Gate Park near 36th Street North. We had to run from there because someone warned us that whites were shooting down Blacks who were fleeing along the railroad tracks. Some of them were shot by whites firing from airplanes. On June 1, 1921, we were found by the Guards and taken to the fairgrounds. A white man who mother knew came and took us home. Going back to Greenwood was like entering a war zone. Everything was gone! People were moaning and weeping when they looked at where their homes and businesses once stood. I'll never forget it. No, not ever!

HAROLD GIBBS, 2002
Born January 16, 1920

I was just a year old during the riot. My mother said she joined the crowd of running Black men, women, and children trying to escape the mobs who were approaching the Greenwood area. She had me in her arms and she was terrified. She said she and the group she was with ran all the way to Claremore, Oklahoma. Then a truck of soldiers came and took them to a detention center in Tulsa. I don't remember which center she said they were taken to. My mother didn't know where my father was. Later, we learned he had been taken to another detention center. After the riot was over, Mother and Dad were reunited. Dad never heard a word from the city about what happened to his wagon and his two horses. He never got a dime from the city from the loss of his "work capital"—that wagon and those two horses!

NELL HAMILTON HAMPTON, 2002
Born March 4, 1911

Things began to get uneasy the evening of May 31, 1921. We saw people with bundles of belongings just walking north, and we saw wagons, loaded with people and belongings, lumbering along the streets, also going north. Around midnight, conditions got worse. We could hear voices and noises of people running down the road near the Midland Valley Railroad tracks; many were headed to the Section Line near Pine, or to the Peoria area, or to parks or to other hiding places. My mother decided that we had better join the fleeing crowd and so we did. Oh what a horrible night that was. There was such a commotion going on—airplanes flying overhead dropping something that set fires, bullets dropping everywhere, smoke, fire, noise, and terrified people running for their lives.

LEROY HATCHER, 2002
Born May 23, 1921

JOYCE WALKER HILL, 2002
Born December 18, 1908

My parents, Augustus and Lois Muster Hatcher, were living in the Greenwood area at the time of the riot, somewhere over by Brady Street. My mother said that the riot commotion reached our house early the morning of June 1, 1921 while we were all sound asleep. The mobsters kicked in the door, threw a Molotov cocktail, or something or other, which set things on fire in the house. My dad told her to run, to join the crowd. He said he would be coming right behind us. But he never did. I don't know if the mobsters grabbed him and killed him right there in the house or what. All I know is that he was missing. My mother never forgot that day as long as she lived. She said she ran nine miles with me, a nine-day-old baby, in her arms. Dodging bullets that were falling near her. After the riot was over, my mother looked and looked for my father, but she never found him. His loss haunted her the rest of her life, and it ruined my life, too. I believe my father was killed in that riot. I just wish I knew where he is buried. I would just like to pay my respects to him.

WILHELMINA GUESS HOWELL, 2002
Born April 25, 1907

VERA INGRAM, 2002
Born March 14, 1914

I have had a lifelong connection with the Greenwood district. My father, H. A. Guess, had a law office on Greenwood Avenue, and my mother's brother was the famous Mayo Clinic–trained surgeon Dr. A. C. Jackson who was so brutally murdered by mobsters during the Tulsa riot. The fact that the riot destroyed my father's office and led to the death of my uncle seemed very ironic to me. My relatives had come to Oklahoma to get away from racism, violence, and death in Tennessee. In fact, Grandfather Guess just barely made it out of Tennessee alive. A Ku Klux Klan lynch mob had come for him. But Grandpa couldn't be kept down. Nether could my father, H. A. Guess be kept down. After the riot, he rebuilt and reopened his law practice. Before he died, Dad said that one of the things he was proudest of was that he represented Black riot victims when they filed claims for riot damages. Some of his records were used by the Oklahoma Commission to Study the Tulsa Race Riot of 1921 when they were searching for documentation to prove culpability for riot damages. I never got over the death of my beloved uncle, Dr. A. C. Jackson. He was my hero.

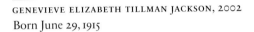

GENEVIEVE ELIZABETH TILLMAN JACKSON, 2002
Born June 29, 1915

THELMA THURMAN KNIGHT, 2002
Born May 30, 1915

I saw what I thought were little Black birds dropping out of the sky over the Greenwood district. But those were no little birds; what was falling from the sky over the Negro district, as it was called in those days, were bullets, and devices to set fires, and debris of all kinds. Mother, sensing the danger, ran out and got me and took me into the house. I saw a truckload of dead bodies being carried somewhere. I was just spellbound looking at those bodies—bodies that looked like they had just haphazardly been thrown onto that truck, with arms and legs just dangling. I got closer so I could see better and I noticed that the faces and arms were Black but that when the arms dangled, a person could see white at the top of the arms. I asked about that. I learned later that those were white men who hadpainted their faces and arms Black so they could get into the Greenwood community under false pretenses. But when they started shooting down the Black people, their game was up and they, themselves, got shot down. Many other Black riot victims told of white bosses who had cots, blankets, and food already in place at their homes and businesses just waiting for their Black employees when the riot broke out. They had to know that the riot was coming.

At the time of the riot, my mother, Maggie Murray, lived at 619 East Cameron Street, off Greenwood Avenue. She lived in a rooming house owned by Mama Lula Robertson. The rooming house was behind the Stradford Hotel, an 85-room building that was burned to the ground. That riot was a terrible thing. My mother lost everything she owned. It might not have been a whole lot but it was hers! I lost everything I owned including my birthday presents which I had just received the day before the riot broke out. I had gotten a new white china doll, some other toys, and some new clothes. It sure did hurt me that I never got to enjoy those birthday presents!

REMEMBERING THE SURVIVORS

LEANNE JOHNSON LEWIS, 2002

KATIE MAY JOHNSON LIVINGSTON, 2002
Born May 6, 1921

At the time of the Tulsa riot, my mother, Louvenia Payne, my older sister, and I, lived with her parents Frank and Katie Payne who had moved to Tulsa from Clarksville, Oklahoma trying to get in on the good life that was supposed to exist in oil-rich Tulsa. Mother said that riot was the worst experience she ever lived through. She said she was just scared to death. She was running in terror with my sister, who was born when Mother was just 13, at her side and me, a three-week-old baby in her arms. She said there was fire and shooting everywhere! People were just running wildly trying to get out of the inferno on Greenwood that day. Some kind of way my mother made it safely out of the inferno on Greenwood. She later went to Clarksville and stayed with relatives there.

ROANNA HENRY McCLURE, 2002
Born February 21, 1914

ELDORIS MAE ECTOR McCONDICHIE, 2002
Born September 8, 1921

My father, William Henry, died before I was born. At the time of the riot, my mother, Lula Row Henry, and I were living with my grandmother, Katie Row, in a house on Pine Place. On the day of the riot, we left home in fear for our lives. We first sought shelter at Dr. Key's house. Dr. Key was a prominent colored physician who lived in a big two-story house on Virgin Street. Then we moved again.

I was a sickly child. I had rheumatism and couldn't walk very well. Grandma carried me in her arms, but she was walking too slowly for me. I said, "Put me down. I'll walk myself!" I remember we all got picked up and taken downtown. Then, later we were taken to a place on 15th Street. The officials in charge put a bunch of mattresses on the floor for the ill colored children.

REMEMBERING THE SURVIVORS

RUTH DEAN NASH, 2002
Born September 9, 1915

I was so traumatized by that riot, I don't remember much about anything, except for my terror. I'll never forget that. When things began to really get ugly on June 1, 1921, an aunt of mine took us to Pine Street where we were to meet up with a cousin who would drive us to Muskogee. Well when we drove down Pine Street to Peoria Avenue, gun-bearing guards met us. I remember one came right up to the car and he had a long bayonet in his hand. I was so scared of that guard and that bayonet that I jumped out of the car and started running back toward Pine Street. My mother jumped out of the car and ran after me. Meanwhile, with all this commotion going on, my cousin couldn't wait for Mother and me. He just slipped away and drove the rest of the family to Muskogee. My mother and I were picked up with a bunch of other Black folks and taken to the YWCA in downtown Tulsa.

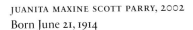
JUANITA MAXINE SCOTT PARRY, 2002
Born June 21, 1914

IDA PATTERSON
Born January 25, 1919

My father, Julius Warren Wiggins, was born April 15, 1888 in Jacksonville, Florida. My mother, Daisy Scott, was born October 16, 1897 in Blevins, Arkansas. They came to Tulsa to get on in the "good life" they heard existed there. At the time of the riot, they lived at 341 (or 404) North Elgin Street. Later, they lived at 707 North Greenwood Avenue. They owned their home, two rent houses, and a grocery store. My mother was a first cousin of Attorney I. H. Spears who survived the Tulsa riot. He is noted for working in a tent "law office" after the riot with attorneys Peter A. Chappelle and B. C. Franklin.

They filed many claims on behalf of Black riot victims and their lawsuit, went to the Oklahoma Supreme Court, and saved Greenwood from being taken over by whites. The unfair "Fire Reconstruction" law of the City of Tulsa was declared unconstitutional. Some of the work of those three dedicated attorneys was used as official documents by the Oklahoma Commission to Study the Tulsa Race Riot of 1921 during the Commission's four years of research, 1997–2001. I am proud that one of those attorneys, I. H. Spears was a relative of mine!

DELOIS VADEN RAMSEY, 2002
Born March 5, 1919

OPHELIA JOHNSON RICHARDSON, 2002
Born February 2, 1915

My father, Hosea Oscar Vaden, owned one of the most popular pool halls in Tulsa at the time of the Tulsa riot. Vaden's Pool Hall was located on Greenwood Avenue next to Art's Chili Parlor. Across the street was another popular pool hall, Spann's Pool Hall. Younger people went to Spann's and older people came to dad's pool hall. Famous people were always coming to play pool at Vaden's Pool Hall. Boxer Joe Louis always came by my dad's pool hall to buy newspapers. Dad sold "Black Dispatch" newspapers and also white Tulsa newspapers. My parents also owned a home on Elgin Street which burned to the ground in the riot. I was too young to personally remember details of the riot, but I heard my parents talk about the riot—how bad it was, how it destroyed so much property that Blacks had worked so hard to acquire.

SIMON ROY RICHARDSON, 2002
Born February 12, 1921

JULIUS WARREN SCOTT, 2002
Born September 23, 1921

On June 1, 1921, when things got so bad, my grandparents sent me on with the neighbors, the Butlers. The Butlers hooked up two mules to a wagon and we headed for Mohawk Park to get away from the fast-approaching mobsters. My grandmother and my cousin, were picked up by the Guards and taken to the Red Cross. Men and boys were taken by the militia to the Convention Center. In all this commotion, my grandmother didn't know where I was. I was missing from her for two days and she was so worried.

She was just sick with grief. She thought I had been killed. A few days after the riot, Blacks were released from detention and most were reunited with their families. But some people were not reunited. Some were never heard of again, like the Butlers who took me to safety in their wagon pulled by the two mules. My grandparents tried and tried to locate them after the riot, and when I grew older, I tried to locate them, but they were never heard of again. I wonder if they are buried in some secret place.

I don't remember anything about the Tulsa riot, but I remember my mother telling me about it. Mother remembers running down the street, six months pregnant with me, dodging bullets that were dropping all around her. She said that it was a miracle that she escaped alive and that I was later allowed to come into this world. She always thanked God for our safety.

VENEICE DUNN SIMMS, 2002
Born January 21, 1905

There had been rumblings on the night of May 31, 1921 that there was going to be trouble in Little Africa. But we hadn't paid much attention to the rumors. In fact, my siblings and I were out in the front yard. We were just looking around to see if we could find out what all the commotion was about. All at once, bullets began dropping into our yard. I was just terrified. When bullets are falling all around a person, you just don't know what to do. I didn't know whether to drop down on the ground, or whether I should run. For a while, I just stood rooted to the ground. I was just paralyzed. My father had heard bullets hitting the roof and sides of our house and he ran out to find us children. He called us into the house. Then he decided we had better run to safety. The mobsters were getting too close. We could see cars full of white men going down Greenwood Avenue, guns blazing and bullets flying at running Black people.

BEULAH LOREE KEENAN SMITH, 2002
Born May 20, 1908

GOLDEN WILLIAMS SMITH, 2002
Born May 20, 1916

Mobsters had knocked a hole in the side of the store and had set it on fire. That was the saddest day of my life. That riot cheated us out of our childhood innocence. My life dreams were destroyed too by that riot. I just loved school. In fact, I had made up my mind to become a schoolteacher when I grew up. But that riot put an end to that. We lost everything in the riot and I had to drop out of school to work and help with family support.

Not only did I not become a schoolteacher, I was not able to even finish high school! What a loss that was to Tulsa and to society. I had such a calling for the teaching profession and I had such love for learning and for teaching. I know in my heart that I would have been a good teacher.

At the time of the Tulsa riot, my mother, Willie Williams Pannell Dawson worked for a white lady, Mrs. Van Horn. During the riot, my mother, step father, and I fled the riot area with a lot of other colored people. I don't remember much about the riot. I do know that our home was burned down and that we were taken by authorities to the fairgrounds.

JAMES L. STEWARD, 2002
Born July 12, 1917

QUEEN ESTHER LOVE WALKER, 2002
Born May 4, 1921

At the time of the Tulsa riot, my parents, Finclair and Lillian Clark Steward, lived at 444 East Marshall Place in a home that they owned. Of course, I was just four years old and don't remember much about the riot. But my parents told me about our terrible experience during that riot. The mobsters set our house on fire. Dad said he tried every door in the house to get us out, but at every door there was a fire! So he knocked out a window pane and put my mother through it. Then he put me through the window into my mother's arms. We joined the crowd of running, scared Black people. My parents told me they saw airplanes flying low overhead and dropping some kind of devices that [set] fire to everything they touched. Thank God, my family survived that riot. My mother always liked to keep notes about things, people, and events. I am giving to the Oklahoma Commission to Study the Tulsa Race Riot of 1921 a copy of my mother's own handwritten account of the riot.

My grandmother used to talk incessantly about the Tulsa Race Riot of 1921, but she has passed on. My mother and her late sister, Corene Love Cummings of Chicago, also a riot survivor, used to talk about the riot somewhat, but not like Grandma. How I wish I had recorded their stories. I want to implore people today to get those stories from their relatives NOW! Don't do like the Love family did. Get your notebooks, cameras, tape recorders, camcorders, slide projectors—everything—and preserve your legacy so you won't have a void in your family history like the one that exists in the Love family today.

SAMUEL WALKER, 2002
Born September 28, 1921

MARY LEON BROWN WATSON, 2002
Born October 9, 1909

At the time of the Tulsa riot, my parents, John and Eva L. Brown, lived in the Webb Hotel which was located on the corner of Greenwood Avenue and Archer Street. My mother's sister, Jeanetta Webb, owned the hotel. I was eleven years old. I remember that we lost everything that we owned in that riot—all our clothes, furnishings, treasured things, etc. My grandparents were Graysons who were Black Creek Indians who had been in Oklahoma a long time. They had nine children and each child had an allotment of land out in an area called Mingo. The worst day of the riot, June 1, 1921, we got early notice that trouble was brewing in Tulsa and that there was going to be violence. My uncle, Bailey Webb, was a Tulsa policeman so he had access to prior knowledge about bad race conditions in Tulsa and his warning allowed us to get out of Tulsa early. So we didn't stay until the situation got so bad like so many of our Black neighbors and friends did. We left early and so we didn't dodge bullets, fire, air planes, and mobsters like so many people did.

MILDRED EVITT WILBURN, 2002
Born January 17, 1921

I don't remember anything about the riot. My memory afterward is all bad. It broke up my family. Mama never talked about it. What I know, I heard from Grandma Liza. My dad, Isaac Evitt, had a business, a club on Cameron. It was burned down. Mama and grandma were Creek Indian Freedmen and had land allotments. My dad forged their signatures, slipped and sold the land to white folks, and opened a new business that failed. He abandoned us and went to California. I never talked about it until my nephew, Don Ross, brought it up in the Oklahoma Legislature. I have been bitter for years. The riot didn't kill my dad, but I believe it took him away from us—and we lost the land that was rightfully our inheritance.

WES YOUNG, 2002
Born February 20, 1917

On the day of the riot, Black men, women, and children who were running from white mobsters were picked up by guardsmen. The women and children in our group were taken to Booker T. Washington High School on the corner of Elgin and Frankfort Avenue. The men were marched to the fairgrounds in the area of 15th Street and Harvard Avenue. The captured Blacks were given vaccines and food. They stayed until some white person came and vouched for them. Some stayed three to four days; others stayed two to three weeks before some white person came and claimed them. The troops put up tents for homeless Black people. Most all the wonderful buildings, commercial and residential, had been looted and burned down during the riot. It was an exception for a building to have remained untouched, though a few did.

As of 2020, there are only two known living survivors of the 1921 Tulsa Race Massacre.

Epilogue

I AM NOT SOMEONE who should be shocked by the photos in this book. Throughout my career, I have studied dozens of lynching photos that include scenes of white vigilantes torturing Black bodies. Nonetheless, when I first viewed images of the Tulsa Race Massacre, I could not look away. I felt compelled to continue looking at more and more photos, trying to come to a clearer understanding of exactly what transpired during the explosion of white mob violence that has come to define both the Greenwood District and Tulsa itself.

There is an eerie quality, even a surreality, to these photos. At first glance, they call to mind photographs of Berlin, Germany, after weeks of aerial bombardment during World War II. In many ways, I still cannot believe what the photos make clear: a residential neighborhood spanning thirty-five blocks was burned to the ground in a matter of hours. Without the photographic evidence, the claim that a community the size of the Greenwood District was reduced to rubble would seem dubious, even audacious. In this way, race massacre photos are portals to the past. They help bring into view aspects of this history that might otherwise be denied or forgotten. Despite the indisputable visual evidence, however, we can never know with certainty everything that happened during the twelve hours of violence that destroyed the Greenwood District. We can never fully know what it was like to experience the terror of witnessing loved ones being killed, family members being interned, or one's community being destroyed.

As I carefully studied the numerous extant photos in preparation for writing this book, it became clear to me that the 1921 Tulsa Race Massacre is likely not only the most destructive but also the most photographed instance of anti-Black violence in American history. The quantity of photos and the prevalence of photo postcards suggests that as whites burned and looted the Greenwood District, they also wanted to document its destruction so that others could witness and vicariously participate in their triumphant defeat of a so-called "negro uprising." This is not to suggest that every photo was taken for this purpose, but it is clear from inscribed captions such as "Running the Negro out of Tulsa" that whites who snapped pictures as Greenwood burned were impelled at least in part by the desire to convey a story of white conquest.

Perhaps the most chilling photos are those that show whites standing over the bodies of deceased Blacks or posing in front of building ruins. Who were the individuals pictured in these photos? Were they involved in the death and destruction, or were they mostly looters or curiosity seekers? Might white contemporaries viewing the photos today recognize the face of a friend or family member? If so, would they be willing to come forward with identifying information for those individuals? Of course, merely knowing the names of white participants and spectators would be far from justice, but it would nonetheless be significant, in that it would remove white anonymity and provide at least a measure of accountability for some whites' role in the massacre. Unfortunately, it is doubtful that we will ever know the identities of the white civilians and civil authorities who participated in the destructive frenzy in the Greenwood District. When it comes to anti-Black violence, justice is too often permanently deferred.

And what about the unidentified Black victims depicted in these photos? Having spent countless hours studying the images, I am haunted by the thought of how afraid and alone they must have felt in their last moments, and by the pain they must have suffered. I am haunted by my inability to discern who they were in life and to know whether their surviving family members were able to provide them a proper burial and thereby gain some sense of closure. I am haunted by the idea that photographed victims were revictimized by being tossed into a mass grave. One hundred years have passed since the race massacre, and yet these questions are more imperative than ever before.

The photos collected in this volume make clear that what occurred during the night of May 31 and the morning of June 1, 1921, was more than a race riot. Uniformed officers of the law and hundreds of white civilians invaded and systematically burned and pillaged the Greenwood District. As Greenwood went up in flames, white city officials did little to quell the violence or extinguish the fires. The violence caused millions of dollars in damage—financial losses that were never recouped. Dozens, if not hundreds, of Black fatalities were likely buried in mass graves. The photos of deceased Black bodies strewn across Greenwood's streets and alleys testify not only to the level of white mob violence but also to the number of innocent Blacks who were killed simply for residing in the community. For these reasons and more, what occurred was at minimum a race massacre, but it could aptly be described as a community lynching. By this I mean that the incineration of every significant structure in the Greenwood District and the indiscriminate killing of its residents was meant to create a spectacle of violence so powerful that terrorized Black people would leave the city and never return. Because of Black Tulsans' courage and resolve, that expulsion was not achieved. Because of their grit and determination, Greenwood not only was rebuilt, but it thrived for many years thereafter. The photos in chapter 6 of Black survivors smiling despite the trauma they endured are a testament to Greenwood's triumph over hate.

While I am saddened by the number of photos that were taken of the race massacre, I am thankful that so many of them survived, because they have made it impossible for the scope of the violence and destruction to be denied. The need to confront the white supremacy embedded in these images, as well as the histories and contemporary realities of racial segregation and anti-Black racism that gave rise to the massacre, is a lesson that I hope readers will draw from this volume. These images should challenge all those who view them to think deeply about our relationship to this history. They should force us all to think about our collective responsibility for the present-day legacies of the race massacre. Current-day residents in Greenwood often remark that they are haunted by the feeling that they are walking atop Black bodies buried in mass graves. The recent initiative to identify mass graves will be important in bringing the community some measure of closure in regard to one of the race massacre's most polarizing legacies. Nonetheless, our collective responsibility must also include vigorous action in regard to reparations for descendants of victims and survivors. Questions of restitution and atonement are never easy, but unless we can address them with honesty and fairness, there is little hope that authentic reconciliation can ever occur. I hope this photographic history of the race massacre will galvanize critical dialogue that can move us in the direction of justice for race massacre victims, survivors, and their descendants.

Chronology of the Massacre

Cartography rendered by Carol Zuber-Mallison
based on Tulsa Race Massacre Maps, Oklahoma Historical
Society, Tulsa Race Riot Commission Collection,
1921–1923/1997–2001, box 16, folder 4

Chronology text reproduced from "Chronological Maps
of the Tulsa Race Riot," in Oklahoma Commission to
Study the Tulsa Race Riot of 1921, *Tulsa Race Riot: A Report*
(Oklahoma City, 2001), following p. 178.

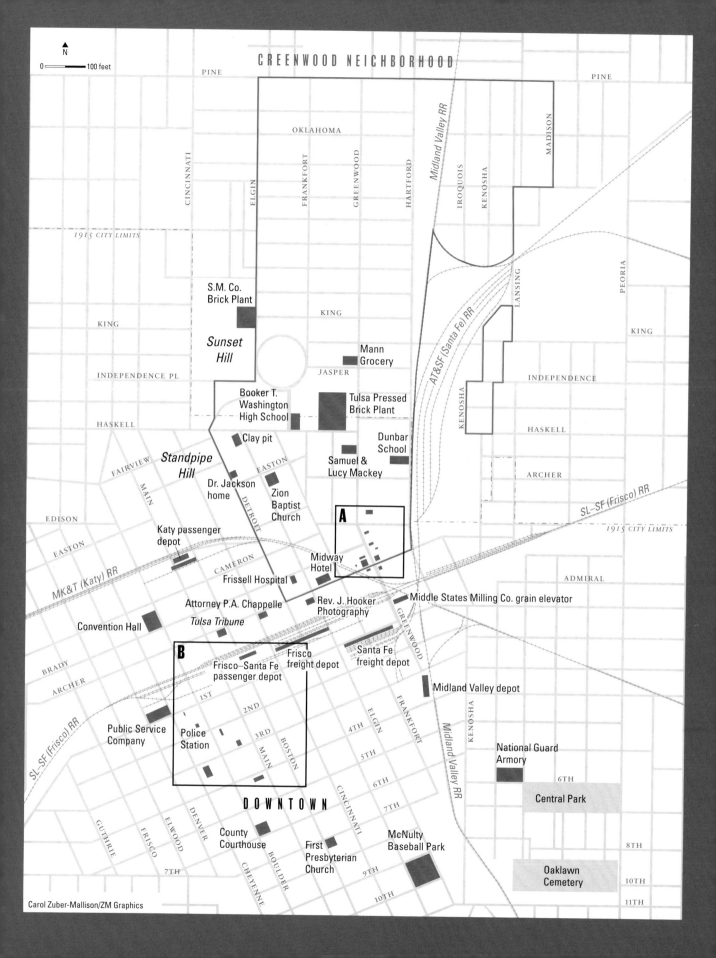

N
0 ⊢——⊣ 100 feet

GREENWOOD NEIGHBORHOOD

PINE
PINE

OKLAHOMA

Midland Valley RR

MADISON

CINCINNATI

ELGIN

FRANKFORT

GREENWOOD

HARTFORD

IROQUOIS

KENOSHA

1915 CITY LIMITS

PEORIA

S.M. Co.
Brick Plant

*Sunset
Hill*

KING

KING

AT&SF (Santa Fe) RR

LANSING

KING

Mann
Grocery

JASPER

INDEPENDENCE PL

INDEPENDENCE

KENOSHA

HASKELL

Booker T.
Washington
High School

Tulsa Pressed
Brick Plant

HASKELL

*Standpipe
Hill*

FAIRVIEW

Clay pit

Dunbar
School

ARCHER

Samuel &
Lucy Mackey

MAIN

EASTON

DETROIT

Dr. Jackson
home

Zion
Baptist
Church

EDISON

A

SL–SF (Frisco) RR

Katy passenger
depot

EASTON

CAMERON

Midway
Hotel

1915 CITY LIMITS

ADMIRAL

Frissell Hospital

MK&T (Katy) RR

Attorney P.A. Chappelle

Rev. J. Hooker
Photography

Middle States Milling Co. grain elevator

Tulsa Tribune

Convention Hall

GREENWOOD

Santa Fe
freight depot

B

Frisco–Santa Fe
passenger depot

Frisco
freight depot

Midland Valley depot

BRADY

ARCHER

1ST

2ND

4TH

ELGIN

FRANKFORT

KENOSHA

Midland Valley RR

SL–SF (Frisco) RR

Public Service
Company

Police
Station

3RD

MAIN

BOSTON

5TH

National Guard
Armory

6TH

6TH

Central Park

7TH

DOWNTOWN

CINCINNATI

GUTHRIE

FRISCO

ELWOOD

DENVER

County
Courthouse

First
Presbyterian
Church

McNulty
Baseball Park

8TH

Oaklawn
Cemetery

10TH

CHEYENNE

BOULDER

7TH

9TH

10TH

11TH

Carol Zuber-Mallison/ZM Graphics

Map 1
Downtown Tulsa and the Greenwood Neighborhood

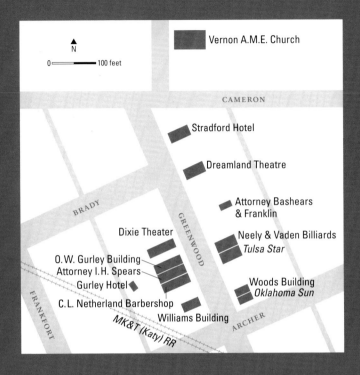

A
Greenwood Business District

B
Downtown Tulsa

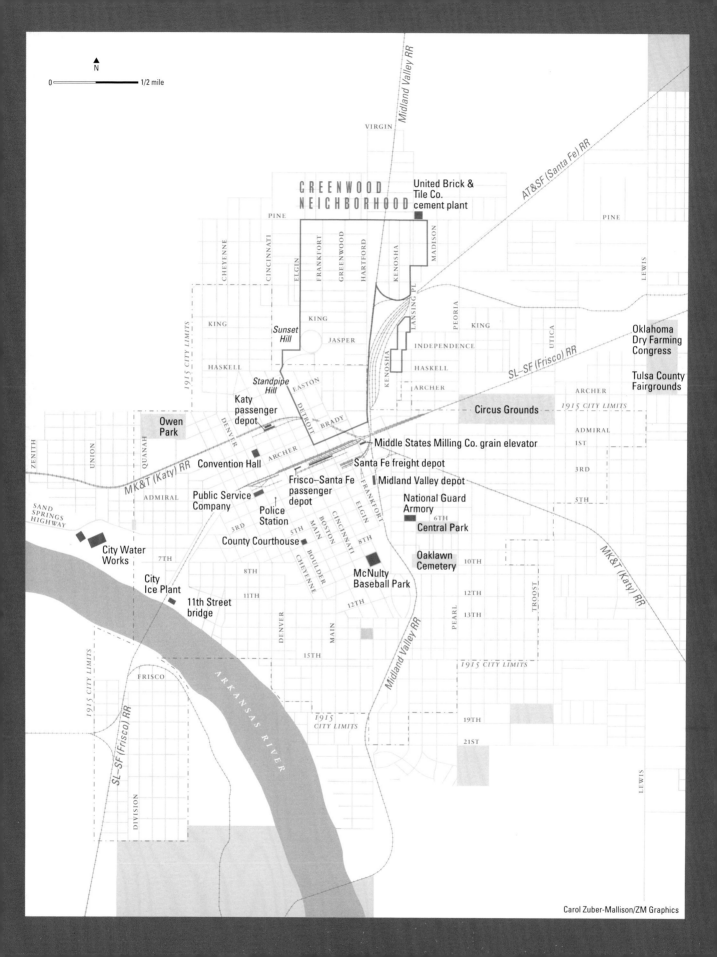

N

0   1/2 mile

VIRGIN

Midland Valley RR

AT&SF (Santa Fe) RR

GREENWOOD
NEIGHBORHOOD

United Brick &
Tile Co.
cement plant

PINE

PINE

LEWIS

CHEYENNE

CINCINNATI

ELGIN

FRANKFORT

GREENWOOD

HARTFORD

KENOSHA

MADISON

LANSING PL

PEORIA

UTICA

1915 CITY LIMITS

KING

KING

KING

Oklahoma
Dry Farming
Congress

Sunset
Hill

JASPER

INDEPENDENCE

Tulsa County
Fairgrounds

HASKELL

KENOSHA

HASKELL

SL–SF (Frisco) RR

Standpipe
Hill

EASTON

ARCHER

ARCHER

1915 CITY LIMITS

DETROIT

BRADY

Circus Grounds

Katy
passenger
depot

ADMIRAL

Owen
Park

DENVER

QUANAH

1ST

ZENITH

UNION

ARCHER

Middle States Milling Co. grain elevator

3RD

Convention Hall

Santa Fe freight depot

MK&T (Katy) RR

Public Service
Company

Frisco–Santa Fe
passenger
depot

Midland Valley depot

5TH

ADMIRAL

FRANKFORT

Police
Station

National Guard
Armory

SAND
SPRINGS
HIGHWAY

3RD

5TH

BOSTON

CINCINNATI

ELGIN

6TH

Central Park

City Water
Works

County Courthouse

MAIN

8TH

Oaklawn
Cemetery

10TH

7TH

BOULDER

CHEYENNE

McNulty
Baseball Park

MK&T (Katy) RR

City
Ice Plant

8TH

PEARL

TROOST

12TH

11th Street
bridge

11TH

13TH

DENVER

12TH

ARKANSAS RIVER

MAIN

15TH

1915 CITY LIMITS

Midland Valley RR

19TH

1915 CITY LIMITS

FRISCO

1915
CITY LIMITS

21ST

LEWIS

SL–SF (Frisco) RR

DIVISION

Carol Zuber-Mallison/ZM Graphics

Map 2
Tulsa, Oklahoma, in 1921

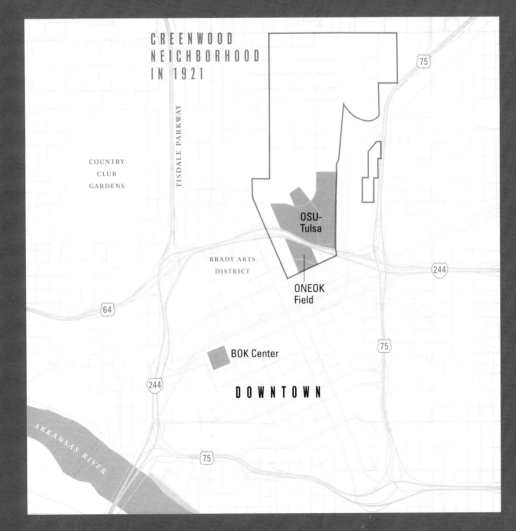

Tulsa Today

GREENWOOD
NEIGHBORHOOD
IN 1921

COUNTRY
CLUB
GARDENS

TISDALE PARKWAY

OSU-
Tulsa

BRADY ARTS
DISTRICT

ONEOK
Field

BOK Center

DOWNTOWN

ARKANSAS RIVER

75

244

64

244

75

75

75

May 31, 1921, 3:00 P.M. to 9:00 P.M.
Partly cloudy • High 87° Low 67°
Sunset 7:34 P.M. • South winds

The African American section of Tulsa contained 191 businesses prior to the Race Massacre of 1921, which included 15 doctors, a chiropractor, 2 dentists, and 3 lawyers. The residents also had access to a library, 2 schools, a hospital, and a Tulsa Public Health Service. The Polk City Directory listed 159 businesses in 1920 and after the massacre, in 1922, there were 120 businesses in the directory. In the City Directory in 1921 there were 1,149 residences and most of them were occupied by more than one person—or even one family; the 1920 directory reported 1,126 residences. After the massacre, the 1922 directory listed 1,134 residences.

The Red Cross reported that 1,256 houses were burned, 215 houses were looted but not burned, and the total number of buildings not burned but looted and robbed was 314. The Tulsa Real Estate Exchange estimated $1.5 million worth of damages and one-third of that in the Black business district. The Exchange claimed personal property loss at $750,000. Between June 14, 1921, and June 6, 1922, $1.8 million of claims were filed against the city of Tulsa and disallowed.

We may never really know what actually happened in the elevator of the Drexel Building on Monday morning, May 30, 1921. A clerk in a nearby store thought there had been a sexual assault. Others believed that there had been a lovers' quarrel between Sarah Page, the white seventeen-year-old elevator operator, and Dick Rowland, a Black nineteen-year-old who worked in a shoe shine parlor one block away. But the most likely explanation is that when Rowland entered the elevator that day, he tripped and accidentally stepped on Page's foot. And when she screamed, he fled.

The *Tulsa Tribune* decided otherwise. The next day, the afternoon newspaper ran an inflammatory front-page article claiming that Rowland had attempted to rape Page. More ominously, in a now lost editorial, the paper may have claimed that Rowland, who was now in police custody, would be lynched by whites that evening. The May 31, 1921, edition of the *Tulsa Tribune* rolled off the presses by three o'clock. Within an hour, there was—once again—lynch talk on the streets of Tulsa.

As predicted, whites began to gather outside of the Tulsa County Courthouse, where Dick Rowland was being held, before sunset. The crowd soon grew into the hundreds. At 8:20 P.M., three white men entered the courthouse and demanded that the authorities hand over Rowland, but they were turned away.

Meanwhile, along Greenwood Avenue, in the heart of the African American commercial district, word of the impending lynching spread like wildfire. Cries of "We can't let this happen here" were heard as Black men and women anxiously discussed how to respond to the oncoming calamity. At nine o'clock, a group of twenty-five armed Black men traveled by automobile to the courthouse. There, they offered their assistance to the authorities should the white mob attack the courthouse. Assured that Dick Rowland was safe, they returned to Greenwood.

The arrival of the Black men at the courthouse electrified the white mob, now more than a thousand strong. Whites without guns went home to retrieve them. One group of whites tried to break into the National Guard Armory, in order to gain access to the weapons stored inside. But a small contingent of armed National Guardsmen, threatening to open fire, turned the angry whites away.

By 9:30 P.M. Tulsa was a city that was quickly spinning out of control.

May 31, 1921
10:30 P.M.

By half past nine o'clock on Tuesday evening, the white mob outside the county courthouse had swollen to nearly two thousand persons. They blocked the sidewalks and the streets, and spilled over onto the front yards of nearby residences. There were women as well as men, children as well as adults. And with each passing minute, there were more and more guns.

Willard M. McCullough, Tulsa County's new sheriff, tried to talk the would-be lynchers into going home, but the mob hooted him down. McCullough had, however, organized his handful of deputies into a defensive ring around Dick Rowland, who was being held in the jail on the top floor of the courthouse. The sheriff positioned six men, armed with rifles and shotguns, on the roof of the building. He also disabled the elevator, and ordered his men at the top of the stairs to shoot any intruders on sight.

Tulsa police chief John A. Gustafson later claimed that he, too, tried to talk the lynch mob into going home. But, at no time on the afternoon or evening of May 31st did he order a substantial number of his sixty-four-man police force to appear, fully armed, in front of the courthouse. Indeed, by 10:00 P.M., when the drama at the courthouse was nearing its climax, Gustafson was no longer at the scene, but had returned to his office at Police Headquarters.

In the city's African American neighborhoods, meanwhile, tensions continued to mount over the deteriorating situation at the courthouse. Outside of the offices of the Tulsa Star, the city's leading Black newspaper, a large group of men and women had gathered, debating what to do, and waiting on word of the latest developments downtown. Smaller groups of armed Black men also began making brief forays downtown by car, both to try and determine what was happening at the courthouse, as well as to demonstrate their determination to whites that Dick Rowland would not be lynched.

A little after 10:00 P.M., when a rumor began to circulate that the white mob was storming the courthouse, a second contingent of armed African American men, perhaps seventy-five in number, set out for downtown by automobile. Near Sixth and Main, the men got out of their cars and marched single file to the courthouse. As before, they offered their services to the authorities to help protect Dick Rowland. Once again, their offer was refused.

And then it happened. As the Black men were leaving, a white man attempted to forcibly disarm a tall African American World War I veteran. A struggle ensued, and a shot rang out.

America's worst race massacre had begun.

May 31, to June 1, 1921
10:30 P.M. to Midnight

Although the first shot fired at the court-house was perhaps unintentional, those that followed were not. Almost immediately, members of the white mob—and possibly some law enforcement officers—opened fire on this second contingent of African American men, who returned volleys of their own. The initial gunplay lasted only a few seconds, but when it was over, more than twenty people, both Blacks and whites, lay dead or wounded.

Outnumbered more than twenty to one, the Black men quickly began retreating toward the African American district. With armed whites in close pursuit, heavy gunfire erupted along Fourth Street. A second—and deadlier—skirmish broke out at Second and Cincinnati, before the Black men, their numbers seriously reduced, were able to head north across the Frisco tracks. No longer directly involved with the fate of Dick Rowland, the men were now fighting for their own lives.

Meanwhile at the courthouse, the sudden and unexpected turn of events had an electrifying effect, as groups of angry, vengeance-seeking whites took to the streets and sidewalks of downtown. At Police Headquarters on Second Street, nearly five hundred white men and boys—many of whom, only minutes earlier, had been members of the lynch mob—were sworn in as "Special Deputies." According

to Laurel G. Buck, a white bricklayer who was sworn in, the police instructed the new recruits to "Get a gun, and get a nigger."

Shortly thereafter, whites began breaking into downtown pawnshops and hardware stores, stealing guns and ammunition. Dick Bardon's sporting goods store, at First and Main, was especially hard hit, as was J. W. Megee's shop, located across the street from Police Headquarters. Eyewitnesses later testified that uniformed Tulsa policemen took part in some of the break-ins, handing out guns to whites.

More bloodshed soon followed, as whites began gunning down any Blacks who happened to be downtown. An unarmed African American man was chased down the alley which ran between Boulder and Main. Near Fourth Street, he ducked into the rear entrance of the Royal Theater, but whites caught up with him inside, where they murdered him onstage. Not far away, a white man in an automobile was killed by a group of whites, who had mistook him to be Black.

Around midnight, a small crowd of whites gathered—once again—in front of the courthouse, yelling "Bring the rope!" and "Get the nigger!" But they did not rush the building. By then, most of Tulsa's rioting whites no longer particularly cared about Dick Rowland anymore. They now had much bigger things in mind.

May 31, to June 1, 1921
11:00 P.M. TO 5:00 A.M.

While darkness slowed the pace of the massacre, sporadic fighting took place throughout the night of May 31 and June 1.

The heaviest occurred along the Frisco tracks. From midnight until 1:30 A.M., scores—perhaps hundreds—of whites and Blacks exchanged gunfire across the tracks. At one point during the fighting, an inbound train arrived, its passengers forced to take cover on the floor.

A few carloads of whites also made "drive-by" shootings in Black neighborhoods, firing indiscriminately into African American residences. There were also more deliberate murders. When a group of white invaders broke into one home, they found an elderly Black couple inside. As the man and woman knelt in prayer, the whites shot them both in the back of the head.

By 1:00 A.M., whites also had set the first fires in Black neighborhoods. African American homes and businesses along Archer were the first targets, and when a crew from the Tulsa Fire Department prepared to douse the flames, invaders waved them off at gunpoint. By 4:00 A.M., more than two dozen homes and businesses, including the Midway Hotel, had been torched.

The pre-dawn hours of June 1 also witnessed the first organized actions by Tulsa's National Guard units. While perhaps as many as fifty guardsmen had gathered at the armory by 11:00 P.M., it was not until after midnight that the local commander received official authorization to call out his men to assist the civil authorities.

Initially, the local guardsmen—all of whom were white—were deployed downtown. One detachment blocked off Second Street in front of Police Headquarters, while others led groups of armed whites on "patrols" of the business district. Police officials also presented the guardsmen with a machine gun, which Guard officers had mounted on the back of a truck. This particular gun, as it turned out, was in poor condition, and could only be fired one shot at a time.

Taking the machine gun with them, about thirty guardsmen positioned themselves along Detroit Avenue between Brady Street and Standpipe Hill. There, they set up a "skirmish line" facing the African American district. They also began rounding up Black civilians, whom they handed over—as prisoners—to the police. Guardsmen also briefly exchanged gunfire with gunmen to the east.

About 2:30 A.M., word spread that a trainload of armed Blacks, from nearby towns, would be arriving at the Midland Valley railroad station. Guardsmen were rushed to the depot, but the rumor proved false.

A half hour later, reports reached Guard officers that white residences on Sunset Hill were being fired upon, resulting in the death of a white woman. Guardsmen, with the machine gun, were then deployed along the crest of Sunset Hill. They were still there when dawn brought an end to Tulsa's longest night—and ushered in its longest day.

May 31, to June 1, 1921
11:00 P.M. to 5:00 A.M.

Even though it was after 10:00 P.M. when the massacre broke out, news of the fighting spread quickly—and unevenly—across Tulsa.

In the city's African American neighborhoods, word of what had happened at the courthouse was followed by even more disturbing news. A light-skinned Black man, who could "pass" for white, had mingled with some white invaders downtown. There, he overheard talk of attacking Black neighborhoods. Returning home, he told what he had heard to Seymour Williams, a teacher at Booker T. Washington High School, who began spreading the word among his neighbors on Standpipe Hill.

But along the southernmost edge of the Black community, the oncoming gunfire had already confirmed that far more than a lynching was underway. While many Black men and women began taking steps to protect their homes and businesses, others sat tight, hoping that daybreak would bring an end to the violence. A few others began to leave town. Some, like Billy Hudson, a laborer who lived with his family on Archer Street, were killed as they fled Tulsa.

White neighborhoods were also the scenes of much activity. As word of what whites began calling the "negro uprising" spread across town, crowds of armed whites began to gather at hastily arranged meeting places. When one such crowd, perhaps three hundred strong, met at 15th and Boulder, a white man standing on top of a touring car told everyone to go to Second and Lewis, where another group was meeting. There, perhaps six hundred whites were told of plans to invade Black Tulsa at dawn.

The Tulsa police, meanwhile, were scattered all over town. Officers had been sent to guard roads leading into the city, including a half dozen policemen who were positioned at the ice plant by the 11th Street bridge. Local National Guard soldiers were dispatched to guard the city water works and the Public Service Company's power plant on First Street.

Word of what was happening in Tulsa also had made its way to state officials in Oklahoma City. At 10:14 P.M., Adjutant General Charles F. Barrett, commandant of the Oklahoma National Guard, received a long-distance telephone call from Major Byron Kirkpatrick, a Tulsa Guard officer, advising him of the worsening conditions in the city. Kirkpatrick phoned again at 12:35 A.M., at which point he was instructed by Governor J. B. A. Robertson,

who was also on the line, to send a telegram—signed by the police chief, the sheriff, and a judge—requesting that state troops be sent to Tulsa. Kirkpatrick had some difficulty, however, securing the required signatures, and it was not until 1:46 A.M. that the telegram was received at the State Capitol.

At 2:15 A.M., Kirkpatrick spoke againwith Adjutant General Barrett, who informed him that the governor had authorized the calling out of the state troops. A special train, carrying one hundred National Guard soldiers, would leave Oklahoma City, bound for Tulsa, at 5:00 A.M.

Any hope that daybreak would bring an end to the violence was soon laid to rest.

During the final pre-dawn hours of June 1, thousands of armed whites had gathered along the fringes of downtown. They were divided into three main groups. One crowd assembled behind the Frisco freight depot, while another waited nearby at the Frisco and Santa Fe passenger station. A third crowd had assembled at the Katy passenger depot. All told, the white invaders may have numbered as many as 10,000.

Smaller bands of whites had also been active. One such group hauled a machine gun to the top floor of the Middle States Milling Company grain elevator off First Street, setting up the gun to fire north along Greenwood Avenue.

Shortly before daybreak, five white men in a green Franklin automobile approached the whites who were massed behind the Frisco freight depot. "What the hell are you waitin' on?" one of the men hollered. "Let's go get 'em." But the crowd would not budge, and the men in the car set off alone toward Deep Greenwood. Their bodies, and the bullet-ridden Franklin, were later seen in the middle of Archer, near Frankfort.

Several eyewitnesses later recalled that when dawn came, at 5:08 A.M., an unusual whistle or siren was sounded, perhaps as a signal for the invasion to begin. In any event, the white mobs soon made their move. While the machine gun in the granary opened fire, the white invaders poured across the Frisco tracks. Up at the Katy depot, the stream of whites on foot was soon joined by dozens of others in cars, heading east on Brady and Cameron.

While African Americans fought hard to protect the Black commercial district, the sheer numerical advantage of the whites soon proved overwhelming. John Williams, an entrepreneur who resided in the family-owned Williams Building at Greenwood and Archer, held off the white invaders with both a rifle and a shotgun before he fled north, along the Midland Valley tracks. Mary E. Jones Parrish, who later wrote the first book about the massacre, also fled. Dodging bullets, she and her young daughter ran north up Greenwood Avenue toward the section line at Pine Street.

Soon, however, other perils appeared. As whites poured into the southern end of the African American district, as many as six airplanes, manned by whites, appeared overhead, firing on Black refugees and, in some cases, dropping explosives.

Gunfire also erupted along the western edge of the Black community. Particularly fierce fighting broke out along Standpipe Hill, where forty to fifty National Guard soldiers traded fire with African American riflemen, who had set up defensive lines off of Elgin and Elgin Place. On Sunset Hill, the white guardsmen opened fire on Black neighborhoods to the east, using both their standard-issue 30-caliber 1906 Springfield rifles, as well as the semi-defective machine gun given them by the Tulsa Police Department.

June 1, 1921
5:30 A.M. to 8:30 A.M.

As the wave of white invaders descended upon Black Tulsa, a deadly pattern soon took shape.

First, the armed whites broke into African American homes and businesses, forcing the occupants into the street, where, at gunpoint, they were marched off to Convention Hall. Anyone who resisted was shot, as were, it appears, men in homes where firearms were discovered.

Next, the whites looted the homes, pocketing small valuables, and hauling away larger items on foot.

Finally, the invaders set the homes on fire, using torches and oil-soaked rags. House by house, block by block, the wall of destruction moved northward.

Some of the fires, it seems, were set by whites in uniform. Eyewitnesses later reported that white men clad in World War I army uniforms—probably members of the "Home Guard," a loosely organized group of white veterans—were observed setting fires in Deep Greenwood. Others claimed that some Tulsa police officers set fire to Black businesses along Archer.

African Americans fought back. Black riflemen positioned themselves in the belfry of the newly completed Mount Zion Baptist Church, whose commanding view of the area below Standpipe Hill allowed them to temporarily stem the tide of the white invasion. But when whites set up a machine gun—perhaps the same weapon that was used at the granary—and riddled the church tower with its devastating fire, the Black defenders were overwhelmed. Mount Zion was later torched.

Black attempts to defend their homes and businesses were undercut by the actions of both the Tulsa police and the local National Guard units, who, rather than disarming and arresting the white invaders, instead began imprisoning Black citizens. Guardsmen on Standpipe Hill made at least one eastward march early on the morning of June 1, rounding up African American civilians, before being fired upon off Greenwood Avenue. The guardsmen then returned to Sunset Hill, where they turned over the imprisoned Black Tulsans to police officers.

White civilians also took Black prisoners, sometimes with murderous results. At about 8:00 A.M., Dr. A. C. Jackson, a nationally renowned African American surgeon, surrendered to a group of young white males at his home at 523 N. Detroit. "Here I am, I want to go with you," he said, holding his hands above his head. But before he stepped off his front lawn, two of the men opened fire, killing him.

Others went less quietly. A deadly firefight erupted at the site of an old clay pit off of Standpipe Hill, where several Black defenders went to their deaths fighting. Stories have also been handed down over the years about Peg Leg Taylor, who is said to have singlehandedly fought off more than a dozen white invaders. And along the northern edge of Sunset Hill, the white guardsmen briefly found themselves under attack. Black Tulsa was not going [down] without a fight.

June 1, 1921
8:00 A.M. TO 9:00 A.M.

Despite a valiant effort, Black Tulsans were simply outgunned and outnumbered.

As the whites moved north, they set fire to practically every building in the African American community, including a dozen churches, 5 hotels, 31 restaurants, 4 drug stores, 8 doctors' offices, more than two dozen grocery stores, and the Black public library. More than a thousand homes were torched, the fires becoming so hot that nearby trees and outbuildings also burst into flame.

The fighting, meanwhile, continued—though now with a startling new development. After the firefight with African American gunmen to the north, the National Guard troops on Sunset Hill then joined in the invasion of Black Tulsa, one detachment heading north, the other to the northeast.

Initially, the guardsmen met with little armed resistance. About halfway across the district, however, they exchanged fire with Black defenders in houses. A second skirmish broke out near the section line, where guardsmen joined with white invaders in assaulting a group of African Americans who were holed up in a concrete store.

As Black Tulsans fled the city, new dangers sometimes appeared. Stories have persisted for years that in some of the small towns outside Tulsa, local whites assaulted Black refugees.

Not all whites shared the racial hatred of the invaders, Mary Korte, a maid for a wealthy Tulsa family, hid African American refugees at her family's farm east of the city, while on the Sand Springs highway, one white man opened his home to a terrified group of Black strangers fleeing Tulsa. When a recent immigrant from Mexico saw an airplane flown by white gunmen bearing down on two lost African American boys walking along North Peoria Avenue, the woman ran out into the street and scooped the children up into her arms, saving their lives.

As the battle for Black Tulsa raged northward, it soon became evident—even in neighborhoods far from the fighting—that on June 1, there would be no business as usual. One white assistant grocer arrived at work that morning only to find the owner locking up the store. It was "Nigger Day," the boss declared, heading off with a rifle in hand.

Downtown, at the all-white Central High School, several white students bolted from class when gunfire was heard nearby. Running north, toward Black Tulsa, an elderly white man—headed in the opposite direction—handed one of the boys his gun, saying that he was finished shooting for the day.

And along the city's southern edge, in the well-to-do neighborhood off of 21st Street, carloads of white vigilantes started going from house to house, rounding up African American maids and butlers at gunpoint, and hauling them off toward downtown.

Even miles away out in the country, people knew that something was happening in Tulsa. Ever since daybreak, huge columns of dark smoke had been rising up, hundreds of feet in the air, above Tulsa.

The smoke was still there, four hours later, when the state troops finally arrived in town.

June 1, 1921
9:15 A.M. to 11:30 A.M.

The special train from Oklahoma City carrying Adjutant General Charles F. Barrett and the 109 soldiers under his command pulled into the bullet-scarred Frisco passenger station at 9:15 A.M. The soldiers, who arrived armed and in uniform, were all members of an Oklahoma City–based National Guard unit. But in Tulsa they came to be known, by both Blacks and whites, as simply the "State Troops." All of them were white.

By the time the State Troops arrived in town, Tulsa's devastating racial conflagration was already ten and one-half hours old. Much, if not most, of the African American community had been put to the torch. Scores and scores of Blacks and whites had already been killed, while the city's four remaining hospitals—Frissell Memorial Hospital, which was Black, had already been burned—were filled with the wounded.

While the majority of Black Tulsans had either fled to the countryside or were being held against their will at one of a handful of internment centers, there were still pockets of armed resistance to the white invasion along the northern edge of the African American district. Perhaps one-third of Black Tulsa's homes and businesses were standing.

The State Troops did not, however, immediately proceed to where the fighting was still in progress. Led by Adjutant General Barrett, one detachment marched to the Tulsa County Courthouse, where an unsuccessful attempt was made to contact Sheriff McCullough. Others began taking over custody of imprisoned African Americans—largely domestic workers who lived in quarters on the Southside—from armed white vigilantes. One account of the race massacre also claims that the State Troops also broke ranks and ate breakfast.

They certainly had the time. After the failed visit to the courthouse, Adjutant General Barrett then went to City Hall, where after conferring with city officials, he contacted Governor J. B. A. Robertson and asked that he be given authority to proclaim martial law.

Remarkably, while the State Troops were occupied downtown, some of the finest African American homes in Tulsa had still escaped the torches of the invaders. Located along Detroit Avenue, near Easton, they included the homes of some of Tulsa's most prominent Black citizens, among them those of Dr. R. T. Bridgewater, Tulsa Star editor A. J. Smitherman, and Booker T. Washington High School principal Ellis W. Woods.

For several hours that morning, John A. Oliphant, a retired white attorney who lived nearby, had been telephoning Police Headquarters. Even though the homes had already been looted, they had not yet been burned. Oliphant believed if a handful of officers could be sent over, the homes could be spared. But, so far, he had not [had] any luck.

Oliphant's hopes were raised when he observed the arrival of the State Troops, figuring they would soon enter the neighborhood. Instead, Oliphant later testified, between 10:15 A.M. and 10:30 A.M. four Tulsa police officers finally arrived on the scene. Rather than protecting the homes, the officers set them on fire.

By the time the State Troops finally marched up the hill, it was too late. The houses were already gone.

June 1, 1921
11:30 A.M. to 8:00 P.M.

By the time martial law was declared at 11:30 A.M. on June 1st, the race massacre had nearly run its course. Scattered bands of whites—some of whom had been awake for more than twenty-four hours—continued to loot and burn African American homes, but many were simply going home. Along the northern and eastern edges of Black Tulsa, where houses were mixed with stretches of farmland, the white invaders had a difficult time distinguishing African American homes from those of neighboring whites.

A final skirmish occurred around 12:30 P.M., when remnants of the white mob converged upon a two-story building near where the Santa Fe railroad tracks cut across the section line at Pine Street. For quite some time, African American defenders inside the building had been able to hold off the invading whites, most of whom had gathered along the railroad embankment to the east. But when a new group of whites—armed with high-powered rifles—arrived, the Blacks were overwhelmed. The building and a nearby store were then set on fire.

Following the martial law declaration, the State Troops finally began to head toward what remained of Tulsa's African American neighborhoods, disarming whites and sending them away from the district. While Black eyewitnesses later condemned both the Tulsa police and the local National Guard units for their actions during the massacre, they largely praised the State Troops.

Yet even with an end to the violence, for Black Tulsans, a whole new set of ordeals had just begun. Thousands had fled to the country, hiding in the woods, while hundreds more had gathered near Golden Gate Park. Homeless, penniless, and often unsure of the fate of loved ones, those who began to venture back to town soon found themselves placed under armed guard.

Convention Hall having been filled to capacity, Black Tulsans were also taken to the fairgrounds and to McNulty baseball park. A few Blacks also found refuge at First Presbyterian Church, and other white churches downtown. Crowds of whites often cheered as the imprisoned African Americans were led away.

White Tulsans as a whole, meanwhile, were sluggish in their response to martial law. While sporadic looting continued along the edges of the African American community, crowds of whites continued their search for African American maids and butlers—though not always with success. Several white families hid Blacks inside their homes.

Additional detachments of State Troops—namely, National Guard units from other Oklahoma towns—arrived in Tulsa throughout the day, and with their help, the streets were finally cleared. All businesses were ordered to close by 6:00 P.M., and one hour later, only members of the military or civil authorities—or physicians and relief workers—were allowed on the streets. Adjutant General Barrett later claimed that by 8:00 P.M. order had been restored. Normalcy, however, was another matter.

For some, it would never return. Upward of ten thousand Black Tulsans were without homes or businesses, their lifetime possessions either consumed by fire or carried away by whites. New struggles—first to get free, then to protect their land, and finally, to rebuild their community—loomed ahead.

Perhaps as many as three hundred Tulsans—some say more—both white and Black, had been killed or lay dying. Even before the sun set on June 1st, the gravediggers were at work. They would stay busy for days to come.

There were a couple of other details. Sheriff McCullough quietly slipped out of town with Dick Rowland. Sarah Page refused to prosecute, and Dick Rowland was exonerated.

SELECT BIBLIOGRAPHY

ARCHIVES AND MANUSCRIPT COLLECTIONS

Greenwood Cultural Center, Tulsa	1921 Tulsa Race Massacre
Library of Congress, Washington, D.C.	American National Red Cross Photograph Collection NAACP Photographs of Race Riots in Columbia, Tenn., Los Angeles, Calif., and Tulsa, Okla.
National Museum of African American History and Culture, Washington, D.C.	
National Museum of American History Washington, D.C.	
Northeastern State University Archives Tahlequah, Oklahoma	Halliburton Collection
Oklahoma Department of Libraries Oklahoma City	Oklahoma Digital Prairie (digital portal, https://digitalprairieok.net/) Tulsa Race Massacre Collection
Oklahoma Historical Society Oklahoma City	The Gateway to Oklahoma History (digital portal, https://gateway.okhistory.org/) LaQuita Headley Collection Ella Mahler Collection North Tulsa Oral History Project Tulsa Race Riot Commission Collection, 1921–1923/1997–2001 Tulsa Race Riot Survivors' Stories (M2006.018-1802.05, box 12, folders 9–12) *Video Tape Transcription: Survivors' Stories,* Submitted to Oklahoma Legislative Commission to Study the Tulsa Race Riot, January 26, 2001
Oklahoma State University–Tulsa Library	Special Collections and Archives Ruth Sigler Avery Collection: Tulsa Race Riot of 1921
Tulsa City-County Library	African-American Resource Center 1921 Tulsa Race Massacre
Tulsa Historical Society and Museum	Tulsa Race Massacre Collection
Tulsa Race Riot Photographs, compiled by I. Marc Carlson	(digital archive, https://tulsaraceriot.omeka.net /collections/)
University of Oklahoma Libraries Norman	Western History Collections: Photographic Archives Division C. B. Clark Photograph Collection: Photoprints, 1832–1925 (1550215-1001)
University of Tulsa	McFarlin Library, Department of Special Collections and University Archives Tulsa Race Riot and Greenwood Community Materials (http://cdm15887.contentdm.oclc.org /cdm/landingpage/collection/p15887coll1) Tulsa Race Riot of 1921 Archive, 1920–2007, compiled by Marc I. Carlson (Coll. No. 1989-004)

SECONDARY SOURCES

Allen, James, Hilton Als, John Congressman Lewis, and Leon F. Litwack.
Without Sanctuary: Lynching Photography in America.
Santa Fe, N.M.: Twin Palms, 2007.

Apel, Dora. *Imagery of Lynching: Black Men, White Women, and the Mob.*
New Brunswick, NJ: Rutgers University Press, 2004.

Apel, Dora, and Shawn Michelle Smith. *Lynching Photographs.*
Berkeley: University of California Press, 2007.

Askew, Rilla. *Fire in Beulah.* New York: Penguin, 2002.

Brophy, Alfred L. *Reconstructing the Dreamland: The Tulsa Race Riot of 1921; Race,
Reparations, and Reconciliation.* New York: Oxford University Press, 2002.

Ellsworth, Scott. *Death in a Promised Land: The Tulsa Race Riot of 1921.*
Baton Rouge: Louisiana State University Press, 1992.

Feimster, Crystal Nicole. *Southern Horrors: Women and the Politics of Rape and Lynching.*
Cambridge, MA: Harvard University Press, 2009.

Franklin, Buck Colbert. *My Life and an Era: The Autobiography of Buck Colbert Franklin.*
Edited by John Hope Franklin and John Whittington Franklin.
Baton Rouge: Louisiana State University Press, 2000.

Franklin, John Hope, and Scott Ellsworth, comps. and eds. *The Tulsa Race Riot: A Scientific, Historical
and Legal Analysis.* Oklahoma, City: Oklahoma Commission on the Tulsa Race Riot, 2000.

Freedman, Estelle B. *Redefining Rape: Sexual Violence in the Era of Suffrage and Segregation.*
Cambridge, MA: Harvard University Press, 2015.

Gates, Eddie Faye. *Riot on Greenwood: The Total Destruction of Black Wall Street, 1921.*
Austin, TX: Wild Horse Press, 2003.

———. *They Came Searching: How Blacks Sought the Promised Land in Tulsa.*
Austin, TX: Eakin Press, 1997.

Grimsted, David. *American Mobbing, 1828–1861: Toward Civil War.*
New York: Oxford University Press, 1998.

Hall, Jacquelyn Dowd. *Revolt against Chivalry: Jessie Daniel Ames and the Women's
Campaign against Lynching.* Rev. ed. New York: Columbia University, 1993.

Harper, Kimberly. *White Man's Heaven: The Lynching and Expulsion of Blacks in the Southern Ozarks, 1894–1909.*
Fayetteville: University of Arkansas Press, 2012.

Hill, Karlos K. *Beyond the Rope: The Impact of Lynching on Black Culture and Memory.*
New York: Cambridge University Press, 2016.

Hirsch, James S. *Riot and Remembrance: The Tulsa Race War and Its Legacy.*
Boston: Houghton Mifflin, 2002.

Hower, Bob, and Maurice Willows. *1921 Tulsa Race Riot and the American Red Cross,
"Angels of Mercy": Compiled from the Memorabilia Collection of Maurice Willows,
Director of Red Cross Relief.* Tulsa, OK: Homestead Press, 1993.

Johnson, Hannibal B. *Black Wall Street: From Riot to Renaissance in Tulsa's Historic
Greenwood District.* Austin, TX: Eakin Press, 2007.

———. *Tulsa's Historic Greenwood District.* Charleston, SC: Arcadia, 2014.

SECONDARY SOURCES

Jones, Marian Moser. *The American Red Cross from Clara Barton to the New Deal.*
Baltimore: Johns Hopkins University Press, 2013.

Krehbiel, Randy. *Tulsa, 1921: Reporting a Massacre.*
Norman: University of Oklahoma Press, 2019.

Madigan, Tim. *The Burning: Massacre, Destruction, and the Tulsa Race Riot of 1921.*
New York: St. Martin's Press, 2003.

Oklahoma Commission to Study the Tulsa Race Riot of 1921. *Tulsa Race Riot: A Report.*
Oklahoma City, 2001.

Parrish, Mary E. Jones. *Events of the Tulsa Disaster.*
Tulsa, OK: John Hope Franklin Center for Reconciliation, 2016.

Raiford, Leigh. *Imprisoned in a Luminous Glare: Photography and the African American Freedom Struggle.* Chapel Hill: University of North Carolina Press, 2011.

Rucker, Walter C., and James Nathaniel Upton. *Encyclopedia of American Race Riots.*
Westport, CT: Greenwood Press, 2007.

Werner, John M. *Reaping the Bloody Harvest: Race Riots in the US during the Age of Jackson, 1824–1849.*
New York: Garland, 1986.

Wood, Amy Louise. *Lynching and Spectacle: Witnessing Racial Violence in America, 1890–1940.*
New Directions in Southern Studies. Chapel Hill: University of North Carolina Press, 2009.